DIVIDE and CONQUER
Book 1

BY François Lemaire de Ruffieu

Published by Xenophon Press LLC

7518 Bayside Road, Franktown, Virginia 23354-2106, U.S.A.

ISBN-10:   0-933316-89-5
ISBN-13:   978-0-933316-89-8

Cover design by Naia Poyer. Cover painting by François Lemaire de Ruffieu.

All drawings, diagrams and paintings in this book are the copyrighted works of the author, François Lemaire de Ruffieu.

DIVIDE and CONQUER
Book 1

BY François Lemaire de Ruffieu

*These pages are dedicated to all my Students
and Riders I have yet to meet.*

AVANT PROPOS

Times have changed. Today, many modern riders have ignored the discoveries of the great riding Masters. Many of those Masters were members of the military. For centuries, the military, for obvious as well as practical reasons, codified guidelines to physically and psychologically train horses.

I have spent several years in the Cavalry. I earned the privilege and was proud to wear the black uniform and golden spurs that are trademarks of the Cadre Noir Riding Masters of Saumur, France. The classical military background that I acquired has always helped me to successfully conduct clinics in the Americas and Europe.

In the following pages, I have transcribed my equestrian teaching into print. To complete this work-study, I have sharpened my pencils to add a few explicit drawings. I have asked my long-time friend, Beverly Pellegrini, to review and retype my prose once again.

Figure 1 – Back to basics

TABLE OF CONTENTS

Avant Propos ix

Preface 1

Introduction 5

Important Instruction Review

    Initiation to Dressage Principles - The Rider's Aids 7

Advice for Trainers and Riders before Beginning the Training Study

    The Rider's Position 10
    Seat 12
        How does the rider obtain a good seat? 13
        Where should the rider sit in the saddle? 14
        How to place the seat in the saddle 14
    Holding the Reins 16
    The Aids 19

Exercises for the Rider 20

    Lower Body Exercises for the Cox-Femoral Joints and Lower Back while Mounted 22
    Exercises for the Ankles 24
    Upper Body Exercises or the Shoulders and Lower Back while Mounted 24

Concepts in Training of the Horse

    Impulsion - Flexibility 26
    Impulsion 26
    Flexibility 27
    Obedience to the Rider's Leg Actions 28
    Longitudinal and Lateral Movements 28

Lesson One – The Learning Phase—Initiation Period ("Equi-robic" Exercises)

    Learning Phase 35
    A.   Transitions Walk-Stop-Walk 36
        Adjusting the Reins 37
        Transition from Stop to Walk 40
        Teaching a Lazy Horse to be Obedient to the Legs 41
    B.   Zigzag (Serpentine or Slalom) 43
        Rein Actions 45
        Direct Rein 47
        Direct Rein of Opposition 49
        Indirect Rein 50

Indirect Rein of Opposition in Front of the Withers.............................51
Indirect Rein of Opposition Behind the Withers...............................53
C. Lengthening and Shortening the Walk..55
D. Moving the Haunches..60
E. Rein Back..65
F. Changing Directions...67

Lesson Two – The Working Phase, Beginning of Dressage, "Low School Dressage"

The Trot..72
A. Longitudinal Exercise: Transitions Trot-Walk-Trot.............................73
B. Lateral Exercise: Zigzags...74
C. Longitudinal Exercise: Lengthening and Shortening the Strides at the Trot.....77
D. Lateral Exercise: Moving the Haunches...78

Lesson Three -- Further Study

The Canter..80
Progression to generate the right lead canter by applying the outside lateral aids....82
Progression to generate the right lead canter by applying the inside diagonal aids..84
Progression to generate the right lead canter by applying the inside lateral aids 86
Progression to obtain the right lead canter from the walk...........................89
Progression for the downward transition from the canter to the walk 90
Phase One. Steady the Pace...93
Phase Two. Shorten the Canter Strides 94
Phase Three. Lengthening the Canter Strides 95
Exercises to Improve the Canter..95
Counter-canter...96

Lesson Four -- Exercises

Exercise One. Transitions, Changing Gaits 100
Exercise Two. Zigzags...101
Exercise Three. Lengthening and Shortening the Gaits..............................102
Exercise Four. Moving the Haunches..104

Lesson Five—On the Bit

A. Lateral Flexion..108
B. Direct Flexion...110
C. Placing the Horse on the Bit...113
D. Placing the Horse on the Bit While Moving Laterally............................113

Lesson Six—Practical Exercises

A. To unlock the horse's poll and spine 118
B. To prepare for the rotation of the shoulders around the haunches...............121
C. To stretch and compress the horse's entire body 122
D. To further unlock the horse's shoulders..123
E. To further unlock the horse's haunches...124
F. To coordinate both extremities of the horse....................................124

G. To individually and then simultaneously move the horse's body parts 125
H. To coordinate the rider's aids by displacing the horse's body parts 127
I. To supple the horse's spinal column and teach the rider to coordinate the aids......128
J. To develop instantaneous response to the rider's aids..............................129
K. To further develop obedience and spontaneity to the rider's aids...................130
L. To improve the mobility of the horse's hindquarters 131
M. To improve the suppleness of the horse's spinal column in both directions............132
N. To prepare for the outside half pirouette 134
O. To prepare for the outside half counter pirouette..................................135
P. To prepare for the inside half pirouette...136
Q. To prepare for the inside half counter pirouette...................................137
R. To develop instantaneous obedience to the rider's aids and instill the idea of full pirouettes 137
S. To prepare for the instantaneous obedience to the rider's aids and eventually to perform full counter pirouettes...138
T. Test longitudinal obedience 140
U. Lengthening the trot on the diagonals across the arena.............................141
V. Improve canter departures...144
W. Spiral in and out at the canter 145
X. To improve and perfect the counter-canter...147
Y. To prepare for the future flying changes of lead at the canter 148
Z. Exercises blending longitudinal and lateral movements to verify the promptness of the horse's obedience and the rider's accuracy.......................................149

Friendly Advice..151

Epilogue...153

LIST OF ILLUSTRATIONS

Figure 1 –   Back to Basics x
Plate 1 –   Louis Cazeau de Nestier (1684-1754)...xvi
Figure 2 –   Dress Code 6
Figure 3 –   Hand and Leg effects.. 7
Figure 4 –   Rider's Position.. 11
Figure 5 –   The Chair.. 12
Figure 6 –   The Fork... 12
Figure 7 –   Classic way 15
Figure 8 –   Modern way 16
Figure 9 –   Holding the reins 17
Figure 10 – Coordination.. 18
Figure 11 – Stretching from the ground 21
Figure 12 – Lower body exercises.. 23
Figure 13 – Toes.. 23
Figure 14 – Upper body.. 25

Figure 15 – Volte, ½ Volte, Circle 30
Plate 2 – *Marquis de Poyanne, founder of the Cavalerie de Saumur* 33
Figure 16 – No point in fighting 39
Figure 17 – Serpentine – Slalom Zigzag 44
Figure 18 – Supination 46
Figure 19 – Supinate indirect rein 47
Figure 20 – Direct rein 48
Figure 21 – Direct rein 49
Figure 22 – Indirect rein of opposition 50
Figure 23 – Indirect rein – neck rein 51
Figure 24 – In front of the withers 52
Figure 25 – Behind the withers 54
Figure 26 – School walk (pas d'école) 57
Figure 27 – Six bipeds 59
Figure 28 – Foot prints good and bad 60
Figure 29 – Hexagon, square, triangle 61
Figure 30 – Moving the haunches 62
Figure 31 – This not That 63
Figure 32 – Rein back 66
Figure 33 – Changing directions 68
Plate 3 – *Gala uniform of the Colonel, Écuyer en Chef of the Cadre Noir of Saumur* 71
Figure 34 – Cardinal points 73
Figure 35 – Zigzag 75
Figure 36 – Loops left indirect rein 75
Figure 37 – Indirect rein 76
Figure 38 – Moving the haunches 78
Figure 39 – Outside lateral aids 82
Figure 40 – Inside diagonal aids 82
Figure 41 – Inside lateral aids 82
Figure 42 – Canter outside lateral aids 83
Figure 43 – Diagonal aids 85
Figure 44 – Inside lateral aids 86
Figure 45 – Canter longer 91
Figure 46 – Activity of the posterior 92
Figure 47 – 24 strides 94
Figure 48 – The classroom 98
Figure 49 – Trot walk stop 101
Figure 50 – Zigzag on straight line 102
Figure 51 – Lengthen shorten 103
Figure 52 – Haunches in and out work on a figure 8 104
Figure 53 – On the bit 106
Figure 54 – Lateral flexion 109
Figure 55 – Direct flexion 111

Figure 56 – Is my horse on the bit?..112
Figure 57 – Dressage arenas...117
Figure 58 – Nose in...118
Figure 59 – Nose out...119
Figure 60 – Nose in and out..120
Figure 61 – Preparing for rotation around the haunches...121
Figure 62 – Counter change..122
Figure 63 – Unlocking the shoulders...123
Figure 64 – Pushing the haunches..124
Figure 65 – Moving shoulders and haunches..125
Figure 66 – Serpentine..125
Figure 67 – Nose inside...126
Figure 68 – Nose outside...126
Figure 69 – Nose inside haunches outside..126
Figure 70 – Nose outside haunches inside..126
Figure 71 – Nose outside haunches outside..126
Figure 72 – Nose inside haunches inside..126
Figure 73 – Coordinating the rider's aids..128
Figure 74 – Suppling the horse's spinal column..129
Figure 75 – Developing instantaneous response to the rider's aids...............................130
Figure 76 – Further developing obedience and spontaneity to the rider's aids..............131
Figure 77 – Improving the mobility of the horse's hindquarters, strengthen stifle joints..........132
Figure 78 – Improving the suppleness of the horse's spinal column...............................133
Figure 79 – Moving the haunches outside...134
Figure 80 – Moving the haunches...135
Figure 81 – Moving the shoulders inside...136
Figure 82 – Moving the haunches inside...137
Figure 83 – Pushing the shoulders..138
Figure 84 – Pushing the haunches..139
Figure 85 – Test on longitudinal obedience...141
Figure 86 – (a) Lengthening the trot on the diagonals..141
Figure 87 – (b) Lengthening the trot on the diagonals..142
Figure 88 – (c) Lengthening the trot on the diagonals...142
Figure 89 – (d) Lengthening the trot on the diagonals..143
Figure 90 – Improving the canter departure..144
Figure 91 – Spiraling in and out at the canter...146
Figure 92 – Improving the counter-canter...147
Figure 93 – Preparing for future flying changes of lead...148
Figure 94 – Exercises blending longitudinal and lateral movements.............................150

*All drawings, diagrams and paintings in this book are the work of the author,
François Lemaire de Ruffieu.*

Plate 1 – Louis Cazeau de Nestier (1684-1754)

PREFACE

"Theory is knowledge, practice is savoir faire *but knowledge must always precede the action. Action must be defined through both knowledge and practice."*

— *Anonymous*

Educating and training a horse is similar to traveling a long winding road. Although the road may be paved with many obstacles, its journey is most rewarding. For many years, I have tried different ways to solve unpredictable situations that horses have presented to me. Discoveries through trial and error, empirical data, discussions with other Trainers and from studying the writings of famous Horsemen have been most enlightening. In many of my clinics, I have noticed that too many riders often lack knowledge of the fundamentals that are the cornerstones of the horse's training. Some methods that I have observed are perplexing while others are pleasing in their softness and subtlety.

We have often heard that one must have done, to know what to do, and to know how to make do. Trainers, Judges and Clinicians often repeat, "You must go back to the basics." I agree that this is great advice, but who teaches the basics and where are they written? A concise organized program is difficult to find.

Great Masters never die. General Xenophon (430-354 BC), Federico Grisoni (mid-sixteenth century), Antoine de Pluvinel de La Baume (1552-1620), François Robichon de La Guérinière (1688-1751), François Baucher (1796-1873), Comte d'Aure (1799-1863), General L'Hotte (1825-1904), Gustav Steinbrecht (1808-1885), and Colonel Alois Podhajsky (1898-1973), to mention only a few world famous Masters, have given us a myriad of clues, but, to my knowledge, no one has really provided a complete and simple, step-by-step progression of these classical and basic methods.

Centuries ago, each European country maintained several Riding Academies. Through war, politics, economics and progress, the use of the horse by the military was replaced with equipment of the modern age, and the number of riding academies declined. Today, there are only four active classic schools.

The Spanish Riding School of Vienna, Austria Equestrian School, completed in 1735 and a jewel of Baroque riding, is considered to be the most beautiful. It is the oldest equestrian institution in the world and continues to train the Lipizzaners and maintains the tradition of ancient Masters such as François Robichon de La Guérinière and Antoine de Pluvinel de La Baume.

The Cadre Noir of Saumur, France was established during the first half of the nineteenth century, although its roots go back to the early sixteenth century. In 1750, the riding school was built in Saumur to receive commissioned and non-commissioned officers with the duty of training within the cavalry regiments. In 1814, the Cadre Noir came into existence. Their horses are mostly of French breeding.

The Royal Andalusian School of Equestrian Art in Jerez de la Frontera, Spain, was re-established in 1973 when few *Haute École* Riding academies remained in Spain. The school was initially a private venture, intended to preserve and promote the Andalusian breed and the Spanish equestrian tradition. In 1975, the school was officially recognized as a protector of Spanish equestrian art.

The Portuguese School of Equestrian Art of Lisbon, Portugal is the newest of the four schools, which was reformed in 1979. The School is responsible for the conservation and promotion of Portuguese equestrian heritage, for practicing, divulging and teaching traditional equestrian art and for perpetuating and developing the breeding of Alter Real horses, descendants from Lusitano purebreds.

All these academies continue to preserve the wealth of knowledge left by great horsemen who uncovered the subtleties in training horses. Their missions are to create riders and instructors who will transmit this knowledge to future generations.

Equitation is the art of developing the horse's willingness to respond to the rider's demand. The results of the horse's education depend on the foundations instilled in the early stages. The horse's first traces of education will remain with him for the rest of his life. In the progression the trainer should be judicious and always remember that horses will have the tendency to do best only what they like. Therefore, horses should be taught in a subtle manner and their work must include many variations and be most enjoyable. Often, one hears that to remedy the horse's mental and physical attitude, it is a good idea to frequently verify and re-verify that the foundations were properly instilled.

Alas, too often, to reach the final goals, trainers are in a hurry, rush, cut corners or ignore details which will become so important in the future. We can evaluate the value of the training by its effectiveness, the means used and the results. There are a myriad of ways to achieve the same results, but the means should never involve force or brutality. It is human nature that riders in difficulty will blame their horse before accusing themselves. We all have noticed that when knowledge stops, anger begins. Horses do not make mistakes, but we do! In the words of Frederick M. Alexander (1869-1955), founder of the Alexander Technique:

"Everyone wants to be right, but no one stops to consider if their idea of right is right."

At the early stages of our equestrian education, we were taught to always check and recheck what we have learned and proclaim to know.

Great Riding Masters have concluded that brilliant training results can only be obtained when the horse is: Calm, Forward, and Straight. This trilogy was in practice for centuries, but was first stipulated with adequate wording by General Alexis-François L'Hotte (1825-1904).

Calm The horse's mind must be truly at peace; disorder or the lack of calm generates imponderables. Calmness is a state of receptivity.

Forward The horse must be obedient to the rider's legs; the horse must always be willing to move forward. The lack of a horse's willingness to move forward renders him in-exploitable.

Straight All of the horse's attributes and body parts must move in harmony and be properly aligned. The lack of this harmony results in disunited locomotion, crookedness, and improper balance.

Calm, Forward, and Straight must always serve as a guideline during the training and the order should not be interchanged. On this subject, all riding schools worldwide agree. These schools diverge only in their style, due to the culture of their own country.

In these volumes, I recapture and explain the foundations provided by the great Masters. I have provided appropriate exercises to recreate, develop, and enhance the horse's natural gaits that should be the common denominator of all riding styles and training disciplines, including Dressage, Jumpers, Hunters, Western, Pleasure, and many others. Book One includes the training progression from the beginning of the elementary level. The training mastered in Book One will be necessary to accomplish the collected and extended gaits, the pirouette at the canter, tempi flying changes of lead, and piaffe and passage in Book Two.

Although different training methods can produce similar results, a rider must know what to do, how to do it, and, perhaps most importantly, why he/she is doing it. The fundamentals are explained in Book One and should be mastered – for the simple reason that what a horse has learned in the early stages of his education will remain with him for his entire life. Later, should a training problem occur, one can always revisit these fundamentals, review, improve, and perfect them.

This work study explains how to **Divide** and **Conquer** the horse's body parts. To be able to properly perform the exercises, the horse should be able to find the appropriate head position independent of the rider. If these exercises alone do not result in the horse's being able to find the appropriate head and body position, I explain the prerequisites to correctly set the horse's head: cession (yielding) of the mouth and the flexion of the poll.

INTRODUCTION

There are no effects without causes.

We have been taught that the same causes create the same effects. In Equitation (a noun derived from mid-sixteenth century French, meaning horseback riding), one may better say, "The same aids always create the same effects." Education to the rider's aids is the most important task. It results in rendering the horse more receptive to the slightest solicitation.

Riders must learn and continually practice how to properly use all their natural aids, i.e., hands, legs, and seat. Knowing the aids, *by heart*, without hesitation, for each particular movement and always applying them with the same consistency, will create the desired movements. At first, these aids may have to be slightly exaggerated to be clear and well-conceived, but with practice, routine and daily repetition, their applications will be minimized and will become more discreet. Eventually, as the horse reaches lightness, the aids will become silent.

The classical definition of a *light horse* is his instantaneous response to the rider's slightest demand resulting from obedience, proper balance, and suppleness. An aid whose application is not immediately followed by an effect or a transformation will diminish in its effect to elicit the desired response.

To accomplish effectively the tasks in riding and training, donning the appropriate apparel will afford comfort and practicality, and is a reflection of good manners and respect to the equestrian sport. On this topic, I will only mention a phrase coined by the *couturière* "Coco" Chanel (1883-1971) that I have reworded slightly for our equestrian purposes: "On a horse, if a rider dresses negligently, she will be noticed by her appearance, but dressed discreetly, in accordance with the sport, the rider will be noticed by the way she rides. *(See Figure 2 – Dress Code)*

Figure 2 – Dress Code

IMPORTANT INSTRUCTION REVIEW

Initiation to Dressage Principles

The Rider's Aids

As a general rule, the rider's hands control the horse's front end (the right hand affects the horse's right anterior, the left hand affects the left anterior); the rider's legs control the horse's back end; (the right leg affects the horse's right posterior; the left leg affects the left posterior); the rider's center controls all.

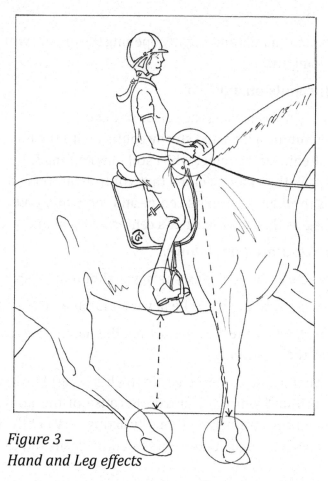

Figure 3 –
Hand and Leg effects

The rider's legs create impulsion (propulsive aids); the rider's hands regulate that impulsion (regulative aids). To successfully ride a horse, the rider should apply the adage from François Baucher [1796-1873]:

"Hands without legs
and
Legs without hands,"

which simply means to clearly separate the hand and the leg actions so that the rider avoids creating confusion and allows the horse to develop in his learning.

The rider's hands (regulating aids) can:

Act: by simultaneously or alternately squeezing and releasing fingers on the reins once or repeatedly.

Resist: by maintaining a firm and steady rein contact with the bit without pulling on the horse's mouth.

Release: by lowering the hands and slightly opening the fingers without losing contact with the horse's mouth.

The rider's legs (propulsion aids) can:

Act: by squeezing and releasing the calves or heels.
Resist: by maintaining a firm and steady contact with the horse's barrel.
Release: by softening the contact while still maintaining it.

The rider's seat is the rider's center that controls all body actions. The rider's hand action begins through the rider's center and torso and ends at the fingers. The rider's leg action begins through the rider's center and seat and ends at the heels.

The rules can be stipulated as follows:

1.) When the rider acts with the hands, she never simultaneously acts with the legs.

2.) When the rider acts with the legs, she never simultaneously acts with the hands.

3.) But, in both cases, when the legs are acting, the hands can resist; and when the hands are acting the legs can resist.

For example, when riding a very electric (high-strung) horse, the rider may ask for an upward transition from walk to trot. Because of the horse's sensitivity and energy the rider might be extremely cautious by acting very lightly with her legs while resisting with her hands to regulate the horse's enthusiasm and to avoid taking off at a high speed, trotting or cantering. If the rider is riding a very "lethargic" horse, the rider should ask for a downward transition from a cadenced trot to the walk. Although the rider should act cautiously with her hands she may be required to resist with both legs to prevent the horse from falling into a lazy walk or stopping.

Acting with the hands never means pulling, but rather, it simply means to close and open the fingers simultaneously or alternately several times, i.e., as in applying anti-lock brakes for vehicles, so to speak. The engineer, Gabriel Voisin (1880-1973), who had invented the ABS anti-lock brakes for airplanes and motorcars in 1929, was a pilot and, of course, a horseman.

• *Nota Bene* •

If the rider uses her hands and legs independently (dissociation of the aids), the rider will learn to measure her actions and become more subtle. Her horse, solicited by more refined aids, will become more attentive.

With a young, green or very inexperienced horse, the rider's leg and hand actions must be clearly defined and divided so that the horse can truly understand and learn their meanings. As the horse's education progresses and evolves, the rider's actions may be demanded at closer intervals, but the hand and leg actions must always be distinctively divided. Harmony between the rider's hands and legs is absolutely essential.

ADVICE FOR TRAINERS AND RIDERS
BEFORE BEGINNING THE TRAINING STUDY

"On a horse, the rider must look glorious but be humble."— Unknown

The Rider's Position

Many great books have been written on the subject of Riding. Some authors describe the physiological aspect; others describe the psychological attitude. All are wonderful and full of truth if their methods are applied as stipulated.

To ride a horse properly, the rider must be well-placed in the saddle. There is an infinite number of good positions for each gait, and each movement has a corresponding series of attitudes. It is the aptitude to quickly be able to switch from one attitude to another with suppleness that constitutes the true riding position.

The rider should be placed on the saddle as if she were standing on the ground with her upper body erect, without rigidity, her knees slightly flexed, her heels directly under her hips and her hips vertically under her shoulders. On the saddle, the rider should have more a feeling of kneeling than sitting. To provide better balance, the rider might spread her toes to enlarge her feet, resulting in more weight being placed on the balls of the feet and lowering of the heels.

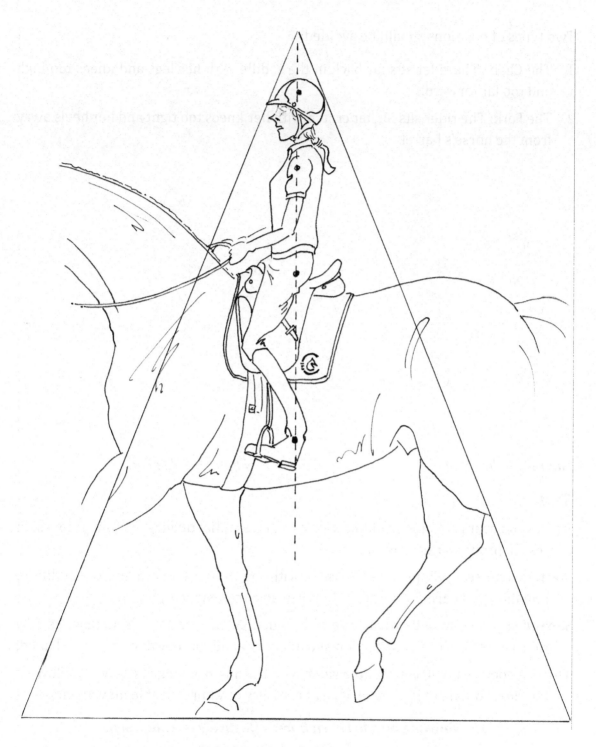

Figure 4 – Rider's Position

Two types of positions should be avoided:

1. The Chair: The rider sits far back in the saddle with her legs and knees too high and too far forward.

2. The Fork: The rider sits on her crotch with her knees too tight and her heels away from the horse's barrel.

Figure 5 – The Chair   *Figure 6 – The Fork*

Seat

A good seat is of primary importance as an essential quality that any rider must possess to properly ride a horse.

First, a good seat will provide the rider with the proper balance and the ability to remain in full harmony with her horse in all circumstances;

Second, a good seat will provide the rider independence of the aids so that she may ride a horse with circumspection and adequacy and thereby develop a good hand;

Third, a good seat will connect the rider with the horse at all gaits, thereby allowing the rider to remain in control of any necessary or unpredictable movements.

The **sine qua non** *to ride a horse effectively is a good seat,
a good seat, and a good seat.*

A good seat also ensures the comfort of the horse through the absence of shocks in his back due to the lack of the rider's suppleness in her upper body. A good seat enables the rider to properly use her superior and inferior aids, i.e., hands and legs.

Almost all problems a rider may encounter while riding a horse originate from an incorrect seat. A wrong or unbalanced seat will result in the horse acting differently by running too fast, being lazy, falling, rearing and even bucking or producing other undesired behavior.

A good seat is the essential condition that a rider must gain to properly ride a horse in any discipline and at any level. Nowadays people often speak about the seat but do not do very much about it. Not so long ago, horsemen rarely mentioned the seat but regularly worked at obtaining a good seat. It was not long ago that I would see riders in the warm up arenas at horse shows riding without stirrups to perfect their seats. Today, I rarely see anyone riding in this manner. What has happened? Is there a new generation of riders born with good seats?

While serving in the Cavalry, my fellow comrades and I had developed a natural seat by riding cross-country without stirrups daily. The Military way, at the time, was *march or die*. Although we encountered many unpredictable situations, we all survived. More importantly, the results justified the means, and the results were noticeable. The training we received shaped our future in the Equestrian world. The Cavalry has been replaced with tanks and other motor vehicles, and a new generation of riders are learning different methods without the benefit of consistency and centuries of practice associated with the great riding academies. Please note that I said different, but I did not say better. What we endured in the Cavalry enabled us to become Centaurs, so to speak.

How does the rider obtain a good seat?

The rider should be as limber as possible. To prepare her body, the rider should not only stretch her muscles prior to mounting but also while riding. First, the rider must learn stretching exercises when the horse is standing and then practice them while walking, trotting, and even cantering. Time and mileage at the sitting trot without stirrups, holding onto the pommel or not, will always be the most efficient route to develop a good seat. In time, as the rider improves her seat, she can trot and canter cross-country and even jump while sitting erect in the saddle (the old jumping style).

Because few riders today practice the sitting trot without stirrups, some may be apprehensive about riding in this manner. Some years ago, I was working with a rider who displayed such fear. After trying other methods, including using a vaulting surcingle, without success, I developed a pair of elastic stirrup leathers. An elastic strip of six inches in length was attached to each stirrup leather. The elastic prevents the rider from putting excess weight on the stirrups, allowing greater suppleness of the lower back, which thereby improves the rider's seat. When these stirrups are used at the posting trot, the rider is forced to use her legs with greater vigilance.

Where should the rider sit in the saddle?

When the rider's body becomes more adaptable to the horse's gaits, the rider should consider how she should properly seat herself in the saddle. To be in balance above the horse's center of gravity, the rider must sit with equal weight on her two seat bones (ischia) as close to the pommel as possible.

The most comfortable place to sit on the saddle is near the horse's withers and shoulder blades. The horse's shoulders are not attached to his spine by a joint but are connected with muscles and ligaments, which implies some elasticity. The shoulders are in the withers area. The pommel of the saddle should be placed on top of the horse's withers. For greater comfort, the rider should place her seat as close as possible to the front of the saddle. By sitting near the pommel, the rider will be positioned above the horse's center of gravity.

How to place the seat in the saddle

Two methods, a *classic* method and a *modern* method, are provided to properly place the seat in the saddle. To accomplish the *classic* method, the rider acts as follows:

1. Hold onto the pommel with one hand.
2. Slightly lean the upper body backwards.
3. Quickly and energetically lift both knees to a vertical plane, simultaneously pulling on the pommel while sliding the seat as far forward as possible.
4. The rider then kicks both legs down and back into place.

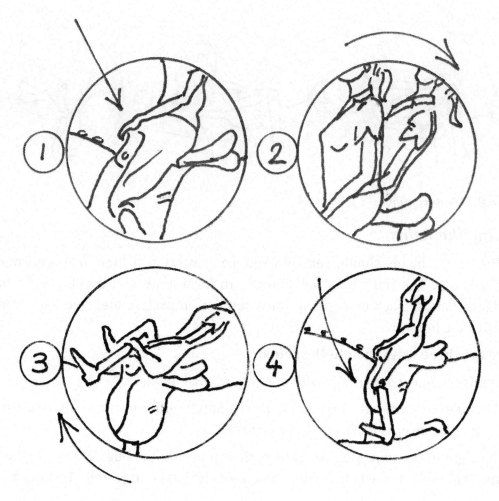

Figure 7 – Classic way

To accomplish the *modern* method of placing the seat in the saddle, the rider acts by: Bringing both legs in front and on top of the saddle flaps. Bending both knees energetically, the rider slides the seat as far forward as possible. The rider then brings both legs back into place.

These two methods can be practiced when the horse is standing still, and then at the three gaits. There are other methods to properly place the seat in the saddle, but they are more psychological than physical.

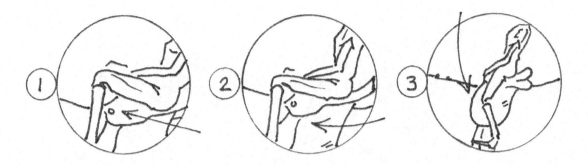

Figure 8 – Modern way

Holding the Reins

The rider's hands should remain fixed, i.e., always at a *fixed distance* from the horse's mouth. The reins must be adjusted to form a straight line from the bit to the rider's hands. Slack or flapping reins send an imprecise message and result in confusing the horse.

There are three ways to hold the reins:

1. The reins are held separately with one rein in each hand.

- The reins come from the bit into the rider's hands either under or above the pinky finger, whichever is more comfortable to the rider.

- The bight of the reins (the free end of the reins with the buckle) come out of the rider's hands and are held securely between the index finger and the thumb.

- The bight should hang on the horse's right shoulder.

2. The two reins are held in the left hand.

- Both reins come together into the rider's hand and split above and under the pinky finger, with the left rein under the right rein.

- Both reins come up out of the rider's hand together and are held securely between the index finger and the thumb.

- The bight of the reins should hang on the horse's right side.

3. The two reins are held in the right hand.

- Both reins come into the rider's right hand with the left rein held between the rider's index finger and the thumb; the right rein held under the rider's index finger.

- The bight of the reins come down out of the rider's hand together under the pinky finger.
- The bight of the reins hang on the horse's right side.

In all cases, the rider's hands should remain soft with the index finger and thumb remaining closed to securely hold the reins. The rider should tighten or soften the contact with the horse's mouth at will by closing and opening, respectively, the other fingers on the reins, as necessary.

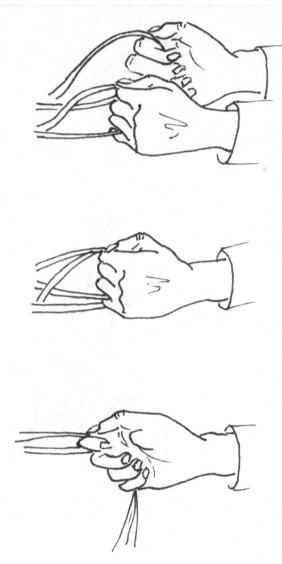

Figure 9 – Holding the reins

• Nota Bene •

The rider must maintain a light and steady contact with the horse's mouth. Although a green horse will be able to maintain a stable head and neck position at the trot, he will move his head and neck up and down as a pendulum at the walk and canter. As the horse learns to flex his loins and top line, the horse's head and neck will become more stabilized at these gaits.

Figure 10 – Coordination

The Aids

In Equitation, to accomplish something beautiful, one must give the impression of acting with the same facility and discretion as artists perform with perfection what they are presenting. The rider's aids must be discreet and applied subtly. The rider must give the impression that riding is effortless, without any constraint or force. At first, the new rider may act with a certain timidity. Then, after learning a few movements, she may have a tendency to overact. In time, through trial and error, she should learn to apply the aids properly and with circumspection. Monsieur Salomon de La Broue (1530-1610) called it "the difficult facility," meaning, that it is so easy that it is, in fact, rather difficult.

• *Nota Bene* •

Examples of the "difficult facility" for the rider:

- *coordinating her right hand with her left hand;*
- *coordinating her right leg with her left leg;*
- *coordinating her right hand with her right leg (lateral aids);*
- *coordinating her left hand with her left leg (lateral aids);*
- *coordinating her right hand with her left leg (diagonal aids);*
- *coordinating her left hand with her right leg (diagonal aids).*

EXERCISES FOR THE RIDER

In the twenty-first century, pragmatic Americans demonstrate concern with their bodies by spending countless hours working out, jogging, studying yoga, Zumba, etc. Shouldn't riders revisit this lesson and apply the same principles to themselves and their horses?

Human anatomy was not conceived to be placed naturally on the back of a horse without effort. A physical education to prepare the rider's body is indispensable. Appropriate gymnastics will warm the muscles, supple the joints adequately to render a rider's body ready for the physical effort of absorbing the horse's body motions at the different gaits. Proper stretching should be painless, enjoyable, and easy to practice. Executed daily, stretching exercises will aid in allowing the body to become more flexible and agile. Stretching will also relax the body, promote better blood circulation, and reduce the risk of injuries.

Stretching exercises should be done slowly at first and then at a slightly faster pace. The suggested warm-up exercises, listed below, should be performed by riders before mounting the horse.

1. Shake each arm and leg independently;
2. March on the spot for a few minutes;
3. Swing arms and legs back and forth;
4. Draw big circles with the arms clockwise and counter-clockwise;
5. While standing, alternately lift the knees to the chest;
6. While standing, bend forward and touch hands to the toes without bending the knees;
7. Standing, lower and raise the upper body by bending the knees;
8. Walk on the toes and heels;
9. Rotate the upper body around the waist several times in every direction;
10. Bend the spine to the left and to the right, forward and backward.

Figure 11 – Stretching from the ground

• *Nota Bene* •

Riders should concentrate on increasing the suppleness of their hip angles (cox-femoral joint) by swinging their legs in any direction, back and forth as well as sideways. The elasticity and flexibility of the muscles around the hip joints will facilitate developing the required seat that is necessary to become one with the horse.

To improve and develop suppleness, fixity, and comfort in the saddle, riders should also practice stretching while mounted on their horses, first at the halt, then at the walk, trot and even canter. All of the rider's body parts should work together yet remain independent from one another.

Correct breathing is necessary. Every movement has a breath. Quietly inhaling through the nose, exhaling through the mouth will ensure relaxation of the body by supplying the muscles with sufficient oxygen.

Lower Body Exercises for the Cox-Femoral Joints and Lower Back while Mounted

1. From the hip, alternately swing the entire leg forward and backward;

2. Alternately and simultaneously raise each leg, bending the knees and firmly kick downward, heels first;

3. Alternately and simultaneously lift each leg, bend the knees and firmly kick backward, heel first;

4. Stretch the left hand forward level with the shoulder, palm facing down. With the left foot kick the left hand. Do the same with the right foot and right hand. This exercise can also be done simultaneously with both arms and legs;

5. While leaning back, pedal forward and backward as if the rider were on a bicycle;

6. While leaning back, energetically swing both legs forward and upward and kick the heels above the horse's neck.

7. Go around the world by swinging the right leg over the horse's neck and sit sideways; then swing the left leg over the croup and sit backwards; swing the right leg over the croup and sit sideways; swing the left over the horse's neck and sit astride. ***[Do this with caution, being careful not to kick the horse; have someone hold the h.orse from the ground - Editor's note.]***

Figure 12 – Lower body exercises

Exercises for the Ankles

1. Stretch the toes upward, downward and sideways, left and right,
2. Rotate the ankles clockwise and counter-clockwise
3. Rotate the ankles in opposite directions: (e.g., left counter-clockwise when the right rotates clockwise).

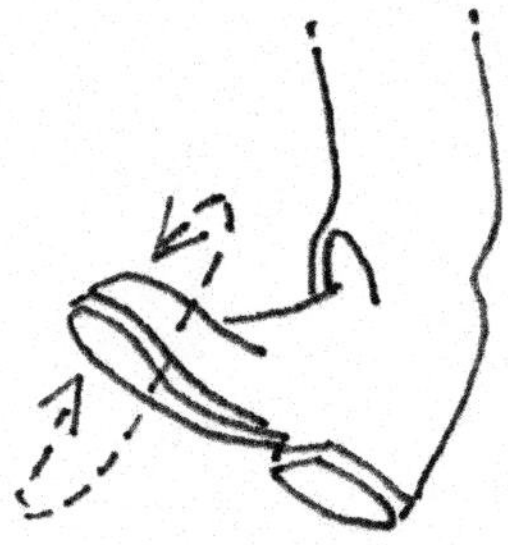

Figure 13 – Toes

Upper Body Exercises for the Shoulders and Lower Back while Mounted

1. With stretched arms, draw large circles around the shoulders clockwise and counter-clockwise, first with each arm separately and then together. While the arms are rotating, the rider should follow the hands' motion with her eyes,

2. With both arms stretched outward to the sides and level with the shoulders, palms up, twist and turn the upper body to one side and the other. At each rotation the rider should look behind herself,

3. Without holding onto the pommel, the rider should lean back until her shoulders touch the horse's croup, with her legs remaining in place and still. To lift her upper body back into place, the rider must tighten both heels around the horse's barrel.

4. Rotate both shoulders forward and backward, first alternately and then simultaneously.

5. Making a fist, the rider punches the air in all directions with both hands, one after the other.

6. Alternately move the left hip forward and to the right, and then the right hip forward and to the left, and repeat.

7. With the legs remaining still, the rider should bring her upper body to an erect position by tightening her heels.

8. Stretch the arms and wrists from the shoulders in any direction.

9. Simultaneously and alternately flex and extend both arms in all directions.

10. Rotate the wrist clockwise and counter-clockwise.

These are only a few of the many exercises one might practice to improve a body's suppleness for riding. Each trainer and rider should practice the exercises that best meet the needs of their own body.

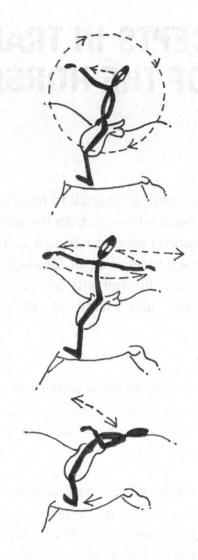

Figure 14 – Upper body

• Nota Bene •

The rider must work the horse from back to front and NOT from front to back because a compressed neck interferes with the muscular development of the top line, deteriorates the natural locomotion and damages the horse's body. The importance is not for the neck to be more or less high but for the gaits to remain steady so that the horse propels himself with his back and posterior limbs. A light and even connection with the rider's hands is essential. The horse's body must remain straight.

CONCEPTS IN TRAINING
OF THE HORSE

The rider must work the horse from back to front and NOT from front to back because a compressed neck interferes with the muscular develoopment of the top line, deteriorates the natural locomotion, and damages the horse's body. The importance is not for the neck to be more or less high but for the gaits to remain steady so that the horse propels himself with his back and posterior limbs. A light and even connection with the rider's hands is essential. The horse's body must remain straight.

Impulsion-Flexibility

Horses' attributes are developed when impulsion and flexibility are combined and work together. While a sport horse requires more impulsion than flexibility, a Dressage horse requires equal impulsion and flexibility.

Impulsion

Impulsion stems from the horse's instinct to move forward with all his energy. The horse is submitted to the precise discipline of the rider's aids to harness this impulsion. Through training, impulsion becomes characterized by the engagement of the horse's posterior limbs and the energy of their thrust. Impulsion is the culmination of combining three elements:

1. Mastering the horse's will or total submission to the rider;
2. Mastering the haunches from which all efforts and movements depend;
3. Mastering absolute respect of the rider's hand, which regulates and guides all efforts.

The horse must respond immediately to the slightest demand from the rider's legs and maintain the activity independent of the rider's help. For example, in a downward transition from the canter to trot the horse must learn to quickly recover his balance and immediately regain the proper activity while maintaining rhythm and cadence.

Impulsion is created by the rider's legs and regulated by the hands. Speed is not a criterion of impulsion. As the horse develops proper impulsion, the horse will regulate and maintain a constant, rhythmic speed.

Flexibility

To harmonize the horse's attributes, the rider, by means of longitudinal and lateral exercises, must develop the elasticity of the horse's muscular system to allow the horse's body to stretch and compress like a spring.

The rider must be aware that a movement poorly executed is not only unnecessary but very often destructive. Through continued practice, the rider must use the aids properly to enable the horse to learn and perform the basic longitudinal and lateral exercises from the simplest to the most difficult and to proceed from what is known to what has yet to be learned.

Flexibility will enable the horse to travel straight. To help a horse travel straight, the formula is simple: ask the horse to turn to the right and to the left many times. The constant turning will develop strength that will enable the horse to better carry himself without falling to one side or the other. Flexibility will enable the horse to achieve the required balance.

• Nota Bene •

Engagement is an equestrian term used to describe the horse's ability to flex his loins and hocks in a longitudinal manner. By practicing upward and downward transitions the horse will begin to bring his hind legs further under his body toward his center of gravity and push himself forward with his hind legs.

Obedience to the Rider's Leg Action

A horse is a very sensitive animal. If the rider continues to act with a constant leg aid, the horse will become desensitized to the rider's legs. The horse must become educated to respond immediately to obey the "whisper" of the rider's legs.

• *Nota Bene* •

Imagine a fly landing on a horse's shoulder. Instinctively, due to a panniculus reflex, the horse will shake his cutaneous trunci muscle to rid himself of this tiny arthropod. The rider uses the horse's sensitivity to a near weightless creature to develop the horse's obedience to the rider's lightest and most subtle demands.

Longitudinal and Lateral Movements

In the following pages, I explain the necessary foundations so that one may achieve success in reaching the final goals: to prepare the horse mentally and physically for the work being asked of him and to allow perfect accordance so that horse and rider fuse into one entity.

The longitudinal and the lateral exercises are the *alpha* and *omega* of equitation. Every horse, regardless of the discipline, should know and be able to perform the combination of longitudinal and lateral exercises developed in this work-study. These gymnastics will lead to the integral restoration of the horse's natural gaits, their regularity, and straightness, which were lost when the horse was ridden for the first time. Throughout the training, these exercises are not an end in themselves but merely a gauge of the success of the training and the horse's suppleness.

Longitudinal exercises develop the activity of the hind legs to compel the horse to better engage and push forward with the posteriors. Remember, when a rider begins longitudinal exercises, the horse may develop some resistance and stiffness in the *rachis* (spinal column) that can pose minor but only temporary inconveniences. The longitudinal exercises include all transitions from the simplest, walk-stop-walk, to the most difficult, canter-rein back-canter and all the variations of speed within the gaits.

Lateral exercises develop the suppleness of the horse's abductor and adductor muscles (that help control the anterior and posterior limbs) as well as the rachis (spine). In the early stages of training, lateral exercises will indubitably reduce the activity of the hindquarters, but, again this minor inconvenience will also be only temporary. The lateral exercises include from the simplest, slightly turn to the left or to the right, to the most difficult, half-pass on a volte with the haunches inside or outside at the three gaits.

• *Nota Bene* •

"Volte" is a noun of Italian origin, volta or radoppio [doubling –Editor's note] meaning circle. This is the only circle that has a name. Long ago, horse masters determined the diameter of the volte to be 6 meters because this is the smallest circle a horse can perform laterally on four tracks rotating his shoulders 360 degrees around his haunches or rotating his haunches 360 degrees around his shoulders. A horse's length, being about three meters, is equal to the radius of the volte. Therefore, this makes the diameter six meters. Nowadays, however, the diameter of the volte is sometimes measured at eight meters because horses are larger.

A half volte is a half circle toward the inside of the arena followed by an oblique line back to the track. It will achieve a change of direction. A half volte in reverse would be the opposite, i.e., an oblique line toward the inside of the arena immediately followed by a half circle to the outside. It will also achieve a change of direction. The diameter of the half circle is six meters, and the length of the oblique line is twice the diameter or 12 meters.

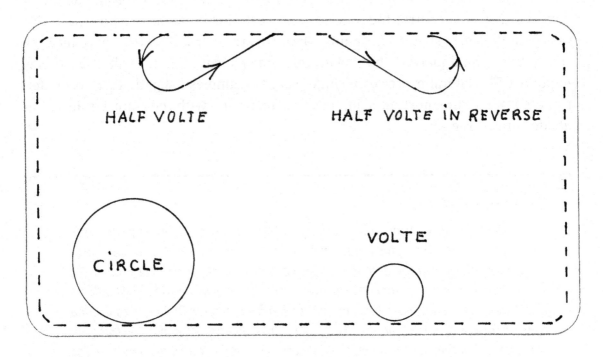

Figure 15 – Volte, 1/2 Volte, Circle

IMPORTANT

To avoid fatiguing the horse, all the lateral exercises must be brief. The longitudinal exercises should always be performed alternately with their complementary lateral exercises. Remember, a spring that does not stretch after it has been compressed for too long a period will no longer be a spring. Longitudinal exercises have the great advantage of developing activity of the hind legs, they have the inconvenience of reducing the spinal suppleness. Complementary lateral exercises develop suppleness but dull the vivacity of the activity. Alternating longitudinal and lateral exercises will produce activity with suppleness and suppleness with activity.

The following training evolution is divided into several lessons that progress from the simplest to the most difficult and from the known to the unknown. To begin this progression, the rider should have a horse that is "green," barely broken, or one that requires retraining.

All lessons should be taught first at the WALK, on a straight line and/or on a large circle, known as the reference circle (about 20 meters in diameter). Each lesson should be repeated in the opposite direction to better develop proper symmetry of the horse's body.

times. If the horse responds well, the rider should repeat the demand only five or six times. If the horse does not respond properly repeat the demands 7, 8 , or 9 times but no more than ten times per daily session so that the horse does not fatigue or become blasé.

Horses will only do well that which they enjoy. With this notion in mind, a trainer should present the work-study in a pleasing manner and with many variations. An exercise that is practiced for too long a period of time may create the tetanization [tense contraction - Editor's note] of the muscle system, or discomfort and possible pain, which will often result in some sort of retaliation.

When practicing these exercises, imponderable situations may result. I will propose workable and practical solutions to resolve these problems. While riding horses, difficult situations will occur from time to time. The rider must remember that an impulsive first reaction will usually be the wrong one. Riders must learn to ignore these first impulses and apply the proper or logical reaction. Riders must study the horse's behavior and learn to understand the animal and avoid making too many mistakes that will only lead to the horse's confusion. The rider must learn how to act and not react to the horse's temporary misbehavior.

Plate 2 - Marquis de Poyanne, founder of the Cavalerie de Saumur [currently known as the École Nationale d' Equitation]

LESSON ONE

Part One. The Learning Phase—
Initiation Period ("Equi-robic" Exercises)

***Divide** the horse's body parts
and **Conquer** them one at the time.*

Always remember the following wise adage from General Faverot de Kerbrech (1837-1905), [*Methodical Dressage of the Riding Horse...*, Xenophon Press 2010]

"Ask often, be happy with little, and reward generously."

This is the teaching part for the rider but the learning phase for the horse. The perfection of each movement will come with daily routine. These fundamental "equi-robic" exercises should be repeated often and in both directions until the horse has truly learned them and can perform them with ease.

The following basic exercises are very important for the future progression in the horse's education. They must be taught with kindness and understanding. Horses are herbivores, therefore, they are not predators. Horses are docile. Horses have an intelligence based on memory and not common sense. (If they had common sense, I do not think that we would be able to ride them.) Horses respond to kindness and not so well to anger and rudeness. To better work the horse's body, it is always wise to alternate longitudinal and lateral exercises.

1. **Longitudinal exercises.** *Transition from walk to stop to walk.* This exercise is performed to develop and improve the horse's obedience to the rider's legs and hands. The exercises develop and improve engagement and the forward thrust of the horse's hind legs.

2. **Lateral exercises.** *Zigzags.* This exercise bends the horse's spine laterally, develops agility of the shoulders, engages the inside hind leg further and propels more with the outside hind leg.

3. **Longitudinal exercise.** *Lengthen and shorten the walk.* This exercise develops obedience to the rider's aids, flexes the horse's spine longitudinally, and improves the engagement and the power of both hind legs.

4. **Lateral exercise.** *Move the haunches sideways.* This exercise laterally develops the suppleness of the horse's top line, allows further engagement of the hind legs, flexes the hocks, and develops the muscles around the stifle.

5. **Longitudinal exercises.** *Rein back.* The rein back is an excellent exercise to unlock and supple the horse's loin area and complements suppleness already achieved from lengthening and shortening the gaits.

6. **Lateral exercise.** *Change direction several times.* Consecutively reversing directions to the left and right incites the horse to bend his spinal column better and further engages the inside hind leg.

Repeat all the exercises of Lesson One above in the opposite direction. With daily practice these exercises should become very easy to perform. They will provide the necessary foundation to pursue the entire education of the horse. Working in both directions will ensure straightness of all the horse's body parts.

• *Nota Bene* •

The lateral exercises are performed for the benefit of the longitudinal exercises. The farther a horse is able to cross his legs, the longer and more elevated his strides will become. Often the tightness of the adductor and abductor muscles will restrict the actions of the extensor and flexor muscles. In time, these exercises should become easier to perform and will be necessary to pursue the superior education of the horse.

Learning Phase

At the beginning, if the horse is very "green," i.e., uneducated, it maybe wise to teach him the rudiments of the "work in hand" (rider being on the ground). This work will have the benefit of familiarizing the animal with the trainer and instills obedience through longeing. Long reining will teach the horse to develop activity in the hindquarters at the early stage. These techniques will be discussed in Book Three.

In this simple progression, the rider teaches the horse to move the shoulders before the haunches. Horses often tend to avoid work with the haunches by performing the work through the shoulders. When the rider has total control over the shoulders, the horse will have more difficulty in evading work of the haunches.

A.   Transitions Walk-Stop-Walk

"Legs without hands and hands without legs" develops obedience to the rider's aids and improves engagement and power of the horse's hind legs.

How does the rider stop the horse?

A.) Think about the demand and be determined to obtain results through obedience. If, for any movement, the rider is not absolutely determined, the horse may take advantage and play with the rider or not respect the demand.

B.) Adjust or re-adjust both reins to confirm a light contact with the horse's mouth.

C.) "Center and grow" *(Sally Swift 1913-2009)* by allowing the body to stretch, vertically, lowering the heels and raising the upper body without lifting the shoulders, and by resisting with the back muscles (abdominal belt and lower back muscles), which allows the rider to shift her weight deep into the saddle. The rider should be resisting with her back muscles as if she were going downhill holding a wheel barrow.

D.) Maintain a steady contact with both legs on the horse's barrel.

E.) Simultaneously act with both hands (close and open the fingers several times without pulling on the reins).

F.) Release the hand, leg, and seat actions as soon as the horse has obeyed, which is known as the "descent" of the aids or the lowering and softening the aids.

Troubleshooting

Problem: The horse does not stop.

Solution: The rider must make certain that the four previous steps have been meticulously performed, including re-adjusting both reins (hands without legs). If, because of poor balance, the horse does not stop after the rider has consecutively closed and opened her fingers on the reins two or three times, the rider should shorten the reins slightly, rotate both wrists so that the palms are facing upward (supinate) and *slowly* elevate both hands in a vertical plane until the horse has stopped. As soon as the horse has stopped, the rider must lower her hands and immediately soften the contact with the horse's mouth. Simultaneously elevating the hands will not only lift the base of the horse's neck but also transfer the horse's center of gravity toward the hindquarters. With practice, the elevation of the hands will gradually be minimized and become less necessary as the horse responds quicker to the closing and opening of the rider's hands.

• *Nota Bene* •

Ms. Sally Swift explained the concept of center and grow by analogy of a spruce tree. "A tree cannot make itself grow; it can only allow itself to grow. So, allow your torso, the trunk of the tree, to grow up while your legs, the roots of the tree, grow down." (Sally Swift, Centered Riding 2, Further Exploration, *page 40, published in the year 2002).*

Adjusting the Reins

The reins should be held in both hands by squeezing the thumb and the index finger while the other fingers have the freedom of loosening or tightening the reins as needed. The action of one hand must not reverse the effect of the other hand. The rider must always preserve the connection or contact with the horse's mouth by maintaining a slight tautness in both reins at all times while riding. The rider must have fixed hands in relation to the horse's mouth. The bit, attached to the reins, rests on the horse's tongue, which is one of the most sensitive parts of the horse's body. The rider must respect the horse's mouth at all times by not pulling on the bit, which may feel like a nutcracker to him and will create discomfort or even pain. Often, horses will find a sneaky way to slightly loosen the reins or steal a few inches to avoid pain or obtain more freedom.

The rider must realize that if the reins are not properly adjusted the horse may not obey with circumspection. The rule is that before acting with the reins the rider's must always readjust them. When the rider shortens the reins, a horse that is not too knowledgable may immediately change the position of his neck, and as a result, the reins will no longer be adjusted correctly. In this circumstance, the rider must readjust the reins again. When the horse has reached a superior level of education and responds well to the rider's legs, the rider will be able to maintain the proper contact only by closing both legs. The action of the rider's leg will instill the forward motion, but a resisting hand will prevent any excess of speed while maintaining tautness in the reins.

The rider must not pull on the horse's mouth. By holding the reins tightly between the thumb and the forefinger (index finger) with all other fingers wrapped around the reins to avoid pulling, the rider is allowed to move her hands in any direction, except backwards, to obtain various responses from the horse. Any backward motion with the hands holding the reins is considered pulling. To avoid pulling, the rider must always have the reins adjusted so that when she wants to act, her first reaction will not be to move the hands backwards to create contact with the horse's mouth. In case the rider is tempted to move her hands backward, she should squeeze both elbows against her body to prevent any backward movement. *I repeat: The rider must not pull on the reins because the horse has an inborn aversion and a total obsession of the fixed point.*

For example, imagine a horse standing quietly in the cross ties in the aisle of the barn. All is peaceful. Suddenly, someone runs into the barn toward the horse's head. Surprised, the horse will instinctively, quickly, and likely violently bound backward as fast as he can, only being restrained by the halter to prevent him from backing farther. The back part of the halter will suddenly create a fixed point on the top of the horse's neck. Horses retaliate against fixed points. To free himself from this fixed point, the horse has two solutions:

- The horse can move forward and release the tension of the cross ties (but this option is not instinctive to the animal; or

- The horse can pull as hard as he can until something breaks, e.g., the cross ties, the hooks, or even the barn walls.

The situation would be the same were the horse to be surprised from behind. The horse would jump forward, but the nose band part of the halter would stop him. To avoid the fixed point of the nose band, the horse would either step back and release the tension of the cross ties or pull even more forward until something breaks.

The situation is the same when riding a horse. If the rider pulls on the reins, pressure on the bit creates not only pain, but a fixed point in the horse's mouth. To avoid the fixed point, the horse will either flex at the poll to release the contact or pull more against the rider's hand, lose his balance, and most likely, run away, which is the method jockeys employ to gallop faster.

Remember, in the equestrian religion, pulling on the horse's mouth is considered a mortal sin. It is punishable not by excommunication, but by running away. The rider must develop firm hands with the delicate fingers of a Swiss clock maker.

Using force against a horse would be the same as arm wrestling with an elephant!

Figure 16 - No point in fighting

Troubleshooting

Problem: The horse does not stop straight.

Solution: Horses do not make mistakes, riders do! The real cause for the horse not stopping straight comes from the rider acting with more strength with one hand and less with the other hand. When the rider does not act using equal pressure in both hands, the hand exerting more pressure blocks the horse's corresponding shoulder and limb on the same side and automatically predisposes the haunches to veer to the opposite side. Technically speaking, a stronger left hand blocks the horse's left shoulder, opposes the front end of the horse with the back end, and displaces the haunches to the right. An equal and symmetrical action of both reins will resolve the problem before the horse learns that he should always stop sideways.

Problem: The horse does not stand still.

Solution: With patience and repetition of the downward transitions the horse will eventually learn how to stand. Patience will be one of the rider's most important qualities in training a horse. If the problem persists, the rider should work the horse "in hand" from the ground with a well-fitted cavesson to reconfirm the transitions and the stops with the voice and to obtain a prompt response.

Problem: The horse steps backward.

Solution: The rider's hands should act more softly. (Remember, the hands should act firmly but with the fingers of a Swiss watchmaker.) The rider should, at first, do nothing, making believe that there is no problem. If the horse persists too much on backing, the rider should then ask for forward motion again and correct the horse with a tap of the whip on the horse's shoulder every time he steps back to avoid standing. Patience and repetition will be required.

• *Nota Bene* •

The horse must stand square over his four feet to indicate proper balance and to be always ready to move in any direction at the rider's slightest demand. The practice of upward and downward transitions will invite the horse to properly position the anterior and posterior limbs at the halt. In theory, if the rider equally resists with both legs in a downward transition, the horse should engage both posteriors. If one hind leg is too far out behind, the rider should close her leg on the same side to invite the horse to place that posterior in the proper position.

Transition from Stop to Walk

1. The rider must maintain a properly erect but relaxed position.

2. The rider should adjust both reins properly to establish a soft contact with the horse's mouth.

3. The rider must lightly but simultaneously act with both legs to create the forward motion, (legs without hands).

4. Immediately, the rider must slightly release the contact with the horse's mouth to allow the walk departure.

Troubleshooting

Problem: The horse does not respond to the leg action.

Solution: A horse must always be in front of the leg, which means that the horse must move forward at the rider's slightest demand from the legs. Being behind the leg is a lack of obedience.

The rider must reinforce the leg action by applying firm pressure, a brisk action of the heels, and/or firmly applying the whip on the horse's shoulder to stimulate action and create the forward motion. If the horse still does not respond, a "Gentle Helper" (G. H.) from the ground may activate the horse with a longe whip applied *à propos* on the hind legs.

• *Nota Bene* •

The whip is considered to be the extension of the rider's legs. When the whip is applied on the horse's shoulder, it will stimulate the forward motion; when it is applied behind the rider's legs, it acts to displace the haunches. I might add that when the whip is applied too far back on the horse's stifle, the horse may be encouraged to buck, but I could allow the rider to make her own discovery.

Teaching a Lazy Horse to be Obedient to the Legs

1. On the reference circle, allow the horse to walk on his own and be lazy.

2. As the rider reaches the center line crossing the circle at X, she will ask for a transition to the trot acting very lightly with both legs.

   a) If the horse jumps into the trot reward him immediately, and repeat this demand several times.

   b) If the horse completely ignores the leg action, immediately reinforce the leg action and even kick with determination acting once, twice, but no more than three times, or use the whip on his shoulder until he runs at the canter or even gallops.

   c) To avoid confusing the horse, do not stop him immediately but allow him to maintain the canter or gallop for at a least half circle.

   d) Return to the walk and reestablish calmness.

3. From the walk at X again, ask for another trot departure using very light leg aids.

   a) If the horse responds well and immediately, reward him with a gentle pat.

   b) If the horse ignores the command, repeat the determined leg action as stated above until he gallops.

4. Repeat this exercise as many times as necessary until the horse understands and trots at the slightest solicitation from the rider's legs.

5. Ask for the trot with lessening leg pressure and repeat the exercise until the horse is completely obedient.

6. For the next few days repeat this lesson by asking for the trot departures from various places.

In the future, every time the horse ignores the leg action, the rider should repeat this important lesson.

• Nota Bene •

The first time the rider acts firmly with her legs or the whip, the horse will be very surprised and may act up. The rider must then stay with him and maintain the course on the reference circle. If the leg action is firm and meaningful the horse will understand very rapidly. In the future any weak or poor transition should be corrected in the same manner. A new transition should be demanded immediately to make certain that the horse has understood.

A horse must be completely obedient to the slightest action of the rider's legs. Once the horse is in front of the legs, the rider may proceed with the same technique using her mind only.

Troubleshooting

Problem: The horse jumps forward too fast.

Solution: The rider must employ leg aids with circumspection and simultaneously, but tactfully, resist with both hands to limit and regulate the horse's enthusiasm to run forward. Repetition of the upward and downward transitions, emphasizing the downward transitions, will eliminate this problem.

• Nota Bene •

"Equestrian tact" is simply the ability to do the right thing, at the right time, with the right intensity, and the right duration. Equestrian tact will be developing as the rider progresses. At first the rider may not act with enough authority; later, the rider may act with too much authority. With practice, trial and error, the rider should discover how to act with the proper intensity to allow circumspection in all circumstances. The rider will soon realize that often "less is more."

Problem: The horse refuses the forward motion by backing.

Solution: The rider should act more firmly with both legs simultaneously, or apply the whip on the shoulder, if necessary. If the problem persists seek the help of a G. H. [*Gentle Helper*] who, from the ground, will stimulate the horse with a longe whip.

Another solution would be to ask the horse to back for a few steps or, if necessary, continue backing until he does not want to back any longer. Sometimes encouraging a horse in his bad habits may create, in his mind, a change of heart.

• *Nota Bene* •

Immobility or a horse refusing to move forward by backing could rapidly lead to retivitee (lack of obedience), which is considered to be one of the worst vices a horse can develop. It must be corrected as soon as possible by re-instilling the forward motion by any means. In Medieval times, a trainer would tie a cat to the end of a long pole and position the frightful cat between the horse's hind legs. Today, the assistance of an adroit Gentle Helper is sought. If the horse kicks at the whip, the trainer must immediately reprimand with ONE firm whipping action behind the croup. This brief sanction should be applied with the most positive intention; the idea is to improve the horse's attitude, not to frighten him.

B.   Zigzag (Serpentine or Slalom)

Riding a zigzag pattern provides two functions:

1. It initiates the rider to the direct and indirect rein actions;

2. It supples the horse's spinal column (*ilio spinal*) to unlock the horse's shoulder one at a time.

Riding a Serpentine Pattern

Acting with alternate *direct reins*, the rider should first lead the horse slightly to one direction and then to the other like a serpentine (slalom) while still following the pattern of the reference circle. This action unlocks the horse's spinal column as well as his shoulders. At the beginning, the loops should be small and wide, moving only two or three steps in each direction, then, as the horse is able to turn better to the left and to the right the loops become increasingly bigger and narrower to gradually accentuate the bend of the spine. When the horse is able to turn to the left and to the right easily, the rider should then first act only with the inside rein as a "direct rein" to leave the track and as an "indirect rein" on the neck to veer back to the reference circle. By veering toward the track, the horse gradually learns to cross his inside foreleg in front of the other.

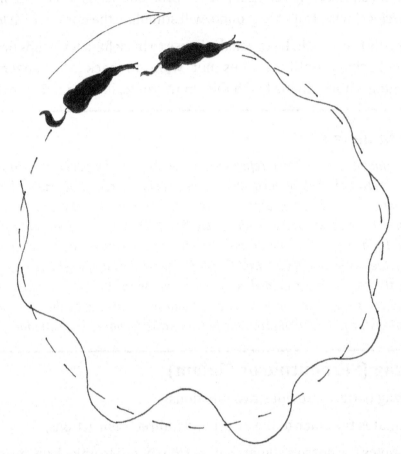

Figure 17 – Serpentine - Slalom Zigzag

The more the horse is able to cross one leg in front of the other, the better he will be able to stretch that leg forward and backward, which will create flexibility in muscles around the limb. To help the horse to improve its spinal lateral flexibility, the rider should discreetly shift her weight in the direction of the motion, i.e., in turning or veering to the left, the rider would increase her weight on the left stirrup and vice versa.

When the horse is bending to one side, the rider must educate her body to always apply a leg at the girth on the concave side of the spine to maintain the activity when necessary and behind the girth on the convex side of the spine to control or regulate a possible deviation of the hindquarters.

If the rider is able to displace the horse's shoulders and or the haunches at will, then, by the same token, the rider should be able to forbid the shoulders and/or the haunches to move when the horse has taken the initiative.

Rein Actions

The rein actions are the means through which the rider may guide the horse. There are five rein actions that are listed below in terms of the functions they perform.

The division of the five rein effects is classical and relatively recent. Classical because these actions were already taught in the XVII century at the School of Versailles in France, recent because they were taught and codified in the mid-XIX century by General de Benoist. [*Dressage et conduite du cheval de guerre*, 1899, Général Jules de Benoist - *Editor's note*.] (The Military, by necessity, has invented 90% of what we know today about horse training.)

There are five rein effects:

1. The *direct rein*, also known as the *leading rein*
2. The *direct rein of opposition*
3. The *indirect rein*, also known as the *neck rein*
4. The *indirect rein of opposition in front of the withers*
5. The *indirect rein of opposition behind the withers*

• Nota Bene •

A direct rein always acts directly from the rider's hands to the horse's mouth and has no physical contact with the horse's neck. An indirect rein *always acts indirectly from the rider's hand touching the horse's neck before reaching the horse's mouth.*

For our present study we will need only the first three of these rein actions. The remaining two rein actions will be used in the future when the horse begins learning the upper level movements.

The rider's aids for the rein actions are presented for turning to the right. (They would be opposite for turning to the left.)

In the following descriptions of the rein effects, I describe a movement by which the rider's wrist will supinate. Supination is the rotation of the rider's wrist, palm turning upward, and the thumb being on the outside. When the rider applies one of the five rein effects, the rider should supinate to easily maintain her upper body straight and erect, which will help the horse to maintain proper balance. Supination will invite the rider to maintain an erect upper body position.

Figure 18 – Supination

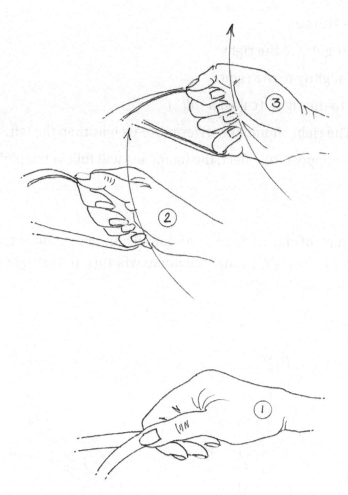

Figure 19 – Supinate indirect rein

[1] Right Direct Rein or Leading Rein (Lateral Effect)

The Rider's Aids:

Hands: The right hand, supinates, the hand moving slightly forward and to the right, away from the horse. The rider's arm remains relaxed with her elbow near her hip. The left hand yields to allow the action of the right hand and then regulates the bend of the horse's neck.

Legs: Applying equal pressure with both legs, the right leg will act slightly closer to the girth; the left will act when positioned a little behind the girth.

Seat: Should be more to the right mainly by increasing the weight on the right stirrup so the rider does not bend her spine.

Reactions of the Horse:

Nose: Turns slightly to the right.

Head: Turns slightly to the right.

Neck: Bends to the right, (called a *"pli "*).

Shoulders: The right shoulder carries more weight than the left.

Haunches: No opposition effect, the haunches will follow the path of the shoulders.

Results :

If the curvature of the neck and the impulsion are sufficient, the equilibrium will be disturbed on the right so that the horse will turn to the right with the horse's haunches following his shoulders.

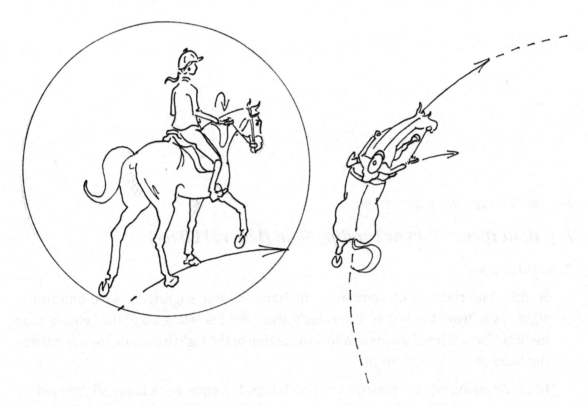

Figure 20 – Direct rein

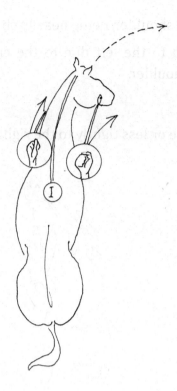

Figure 21 – Direct rein

[2] The Right Direct Rein of Opposition (Lateral Effect)

The Rider's Aids

Hands: The right hand supinates and moves slightly to the right and away from the horse. The right hand acts lightly, creating an increase in resistance from front to back and parallel to the horse's body. The left hand yields and regulates the action.

Legs: The rider's right leg pushes the horse's haunches to the left; the rider's left leg regulates the rate of displacement of the haunches,

Seat: The rider's seat will be positioned slightly to the left (by increasing her weight on the left stirrup).

Reactions of the Horse

Nose: Moves to the right and back.

Head: Moves to the right and back.

Neck: Curved to the right,

Shoulders: The right shoulder, being heavily charged, will move to the right,

Haunches: Displaced to the left due to the curving of the spinal column and opposite to the left shoulder.

Results

The horse turns more or less tightly to the right, or pivots on the spot.

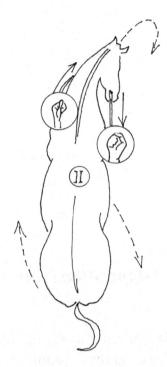

Figure 22 – Indirect rein of opposition

[3] The Right Indirect Rein or Neck Rein (Diagonal Effect)

The Rider's Aids

Hands: The right hand supinates, acting slightly forward and to the left, without crossing over the crest of the neck. The left hand yields and is positioned a little lower than the right hand.

Legs: The rider's right leg predominates slightly to accentuate the movement. The left leg is passive.

Seat: Positioned slightly to the left seat bone by increasing the weight on the left stirrup.

Reactions of the Horse

Nose: Slightly to the right (counter bend).

Head: The poll will slightly tilt to the left.

Neck: Bend slightly to the right.

Shoulders: The left shoulder is slightly more burdened.

Haunches: No effect of opposition; the haunches will follow the shoulders.

Results

The horse's shoulder veers to the left with the haunches following the forehand.

Figure 23 – Indirect rein – neck rein

[4] The Right Indirect Rein of Opposition in Front of the Withers

The Rider's Aids

Hands: The right hand supinates and acts from right to left in front of the horse's withers. The left hand yields by moving forward and lower, to then regulate the action of the right hand.

Legs: The rider's right leg sustains; the left leg acts to push the haunches to the right.

Seat: The rider will have more weight on the left seat bone, thereby increasing the weight on the left stirrup.

Reactions of the Horse

Nose: To the right and back

Head: To the right and back

Neck: Concave on the right

Shoulders: The left shoulder will bear more weight.

Haunches: The haunches will be displaced to the right in opposition to the shoulder, which will be moving to the left.

Results

The horse's equilibrium is disturbed toward the back and to the left because of the weight increase on the left shoulder and the haunches deviating to the right. The horse will turn to the left pivoting around the haunches if the horse is in continual motion. If the horse is at a standstill or is moving very slowly, the horse will move backwards.

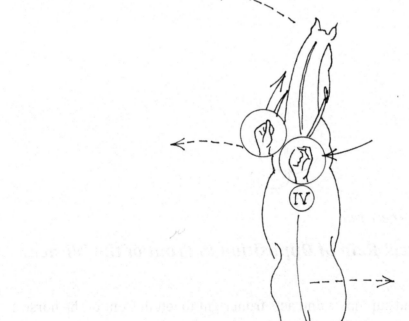

Figure 24 – In front of the withers

[5] The Right Rein of Opposition Behind the Withers

The Rider's Aids

Hands: The right hand acts from right to left behind the withers and the shoulders. The left hand yields by moving forward and lower, regulating the action of the right hand.

Legs: The right leg acts slightly behind the girth to push the haunches to the left and to support the movement. The left leg maintains the impulsion.

Seat: The rider's seat will be positioned more to the left thereby increasing the weight on the left stirrup.

Reactions of the Horse

Nose: Move to the right and back

Head: Move to the right and back

Neck: Concave on the right.

Shoulders: The left shoulder will bear more weight

Haunches: The haunches will deviate diagonally to the left

Results

The curvature of the neck to the right will increase the weight on the horse's left shoulder and left haunch. The right rein, acting through the horse's center of gravity, will displace the horse's entire body to the left.

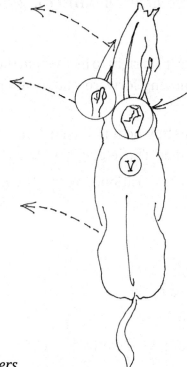

Figure 25 – Behind the withers

• *Nota Bene* •

A bend (pli) is a slight rotation of the horse's head at the poll in the direction of the motion. A counter bend is a slight rotation of the horse's head at the poll in the opposite direction of the bend in the horse's neck. Tracking to the right, the horse's nose will be to the left; tracking to the right, the horse's nose will point to the left. The rider's hands must never cross over the crest of the horse's neck. The rider's right hand belongs to the right side of the horse and vice versa for the left hand.

To straighten the horse's body while going forward or backward, the rider should move the head in rapport to the neck, the neck in rapport to the shoulder, and the shoulder-in rapport to the haunches. Consequently, to straighten the horse's body, the rider should ALWAYS place the horse's shoulder-in front of the haunches and not the haunches behind the horse's shoulders to avoid disorganizing the gait.

Straightness is most important for the symmetry of the horse.

Troubleshooting

Problem: The horse does not turn in either direction or will turn only to one side.

Solution: The rider must first readjust or shorten the active direct rein and, in a vertical plane, progressively elevate the active hand, palm facing up (supinating), until the horse has bent the neck and begins turning. Increasing the leg actions will also be necessary. As soon as the horse begins to respond by turning, the rider must immediately lower the active hand as a reward to the horse. After several days of practice, if no improvement is apparent, the rider or a G. H. from the ground can lead the horse to progressively turn tighter to the left and to the right for a few minutes each day.

If the horse does not respond well to the active indirect rein, the rider should try to act by bringing the active hand more forward toward the middle of the horse's neck to determine where the horse is more sensitive. The other hand may help by leading the horse in the desired direction. To accentuate the aids, the rider can also slide her seat slightly back to lighten her weight on the horse's forehand.

With practice the action of this indirect rein will be applied gradually closer to the rider's body to finally become imperceptible. If the horse does not respond to this rein action, the rider should return to applying the leading direct reins, both left and right, until the horse becomes more adept at turning in either direction.

C.   *Lengthening and Shortening the Walk*

This exercise is demanded to confirm the obedience to the rider's legs and hands and to improve the thrust and the engagement of the horse's hind legs. The exercise will allow the spinal column to flex and extend in a longitudinal direction. At first, this transition may not be very easy to obtain. In the beginning, the rhythm and the cadence will be altered. After several sessions, however, the horse will be able to easily change rhythm while maintaining the same cadence/tempo.

How does the rider lengthen and shorten the walk?

To lengthen the strides, the rider will act simultaneously with both legs while releasing the hands to allow the action. The best way would be to equally squeeze both legs for a period of two or three strides and then allow the horse to move forward. To shorten the strides the rider will cease the stimulating leg action and resist with her back muscles, while alternating the closing and opening of the fingers on the reins in both hands. To be accurate, the rider should be acting by closing and opening the fingers with the right hand when the horse's right shoulder is moving backwards and vice versa for the left. These brief actions will prolong the time that the horse's foot is on the ground and thereby slow the gait. In the event that the horse slowing too much to stop, the rider will, indeed, act with both legs immediately to re-create the forward movement. With practice, the horse will be able to slow and then hasten the gait as well as switch more promptly from the rhythm of lengthening and shortening the stride while maintaining the same tempo. This lengthening and shortening exercise also will provide to the rider another opportunity to apply the sacrosanct concept of François Baucher; legs without hands, to lengthen the strides and hands without legs, to shorten the stride.

Troubleshooting

Problem: The horse cannot or does not want to change the length of stride.

Solution: The rider's first reaction should be to go back in the training progression and improve Phase A of this lesson: transitions walk-stop-walk. If the horse can easily switch from walk to stop to walk it is indubitable that soon he will be able to switch speed within the walk because to stop, the horse must first slow the gait. Daily practice will render the exercise possible with greater amplification.

• Nota Bene •

When the horse lengthens the stride of the walk, he will have the tendency to lateralize the order of foot falls. When the rider reduces the speed, the horse will have the tendency to diagonalize the order of foot falls.

Problem: The horse changes the tempo while changing speed.

Solution: Asking the horse a myriad of upward and downward transitions will progressively incite the horse to maintain a steady tempo. A slow horse will anticipate the upward transition and walk with more energy, and an electric horse will anticipate the downward transition and walk at a slower pace. Therefore, to maintain the same pace, the rider should change gaits and speed often. As the horse becomes better able to walk at a slower pace while maintaining the same tempo (the rider may alternatively activate both legs while maintaining the same speed), he will synchronize his legs more diagonally than laterally and will raise and steady the base of his neck, improve the direct flexion at the poll and flex his loins. The result will show a more elegant walk with long sliding steps, which later may develop into the "school walk," similar to a British foot soldier (royal horse Guards at the palace) walking in a parade.

• *Nota Bene* •

In public presentations, the school walk is the privilege of the Ecuyer en Chef of the Cadre Noir.

Figure 26 – School walk (pas d'école)

Troubleshooting

Problem: The horse is twisting his body while slowing the pace.

Solution: At first this is a normal reaction. Daily practice will render the horse's muscles more flexible and eliminate this temporary lack of straightness.

• *Nota Bene* •

A horse is said to be straight when the legs of each lateral biped are parallel, i.e., the right hind foot and the right front foot are in line and equidistant from the left hind and the left front so that the hind legs are following the path of their respective front legs. To straighten the horse's body, the rider must be properly balanced in her seat, maintain her shoulders at the same level with equal contact in both reins. An effective way to straighten a green horse is to switch the diagonal biped at the rising trot every 4 or 5 strides. When the horse is in a crooked position, the rider must always correct it by placing the horse's shoulders in front of the haunches. Moving the haunches to straighten the horse's body will most likely result in a disunited gait.

Even though the horse is a quadruped, horsemen have divided the horse's legs into bipeds to better explain the footfalls. The horse has six bipeds:

1. the front biped: the right and the left front legs;
2. the back biped: the right and the left back legs;
3. the right lateral biped: the right front leg and the right hind leg;
4. the left lateral biped: the left front leg and left hind leg;
5. the right diagonal biped: the right front leg and the left back leg; and
6. the left diagonal biped: the left front leg and the right hind leg.

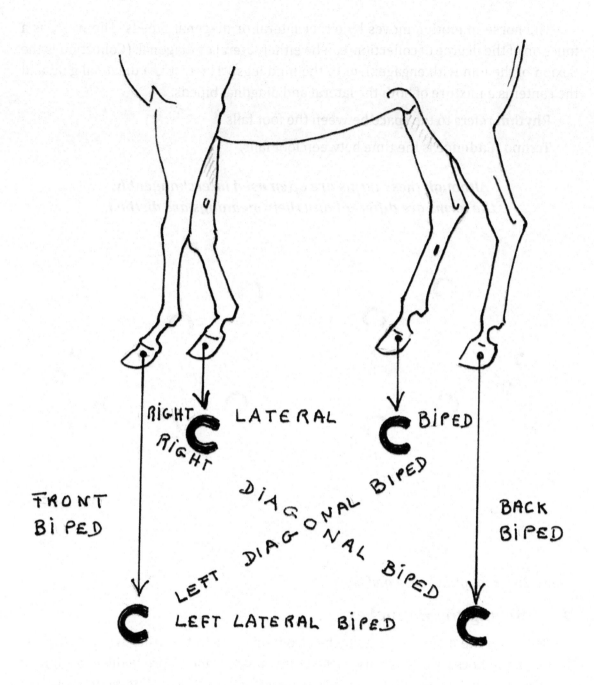

POLYGON OF SUSTENTATION

Figure 27 – Six bipeds

The horse in motion moves by either lateral or diagonal bipeds. The walk, as a function of the degree of collection, can be either lateral or diagonal. (Collection is the flexion of the loin with engagement of the hind legs.) The trot is a diagonal gait, and the canter is a mixture of both the lateral and diagonal bipeds.

Rhythm refers to the space between the foot falls.

Tempo/Cadence is the time between foot falls.

Although these terms are often used interchangeably,
the terms are different and their meanings are distinct.

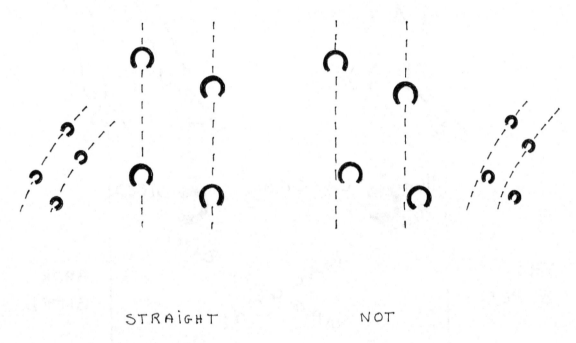

STRAIGHT   NOT

Figure 28 – Foot prints good and bad

D.   *Moving the Haunches*

The ability to displace the haunches from one side to the other will develop the flexion of the hocks, the elasticity of the stifle muscles, and improve the engagement of the hind legs. Moving the hindquarters laterally will incite the horse to cross one hind leg in front of the other, which will unlock the lateral abductor and adductor muscles, strengthen the stifles, and develop thrusting power.

To succeed, it is best to first teach the horse "in hand" from the ground.

How does the mounted rider move the horse's haunches?

1. Mounted, the rider should first follow the pattern of a hexagon, stopping at each point of the six sides. The rider should act with an inside leg behind the girth to displace the horse's haunches one step to the outside of the hexagon pattern. The rider should walk to the end of the next segment, stop, and again, move the haunches one step to the outside. The rider should continue this pattern for each segment of the hexagon.

2. Following the pattern of a square, the rider should proceed in the same manner as indicated above, except that at each corner, after stopping, the rider should ask the horse to move two steps to the outside.

3. Following the pattern of a triangle the rider should proceed in the same manner, but instead, ask the horse for haunches to the outside for three steps.

4. Working on a straight line, the rider should ask the horse to rotate his haunches 180 degrees around the shoulders in four steps to the outside, until the horse is on a straight line and facing in the opposite direction.

5. The rider should continue this pattern to create a three-quarter circle, and finally a full turn.

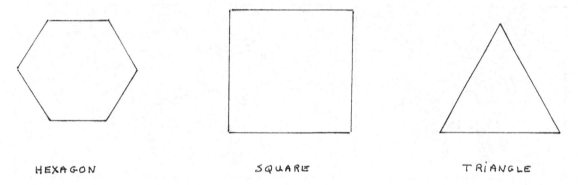

HEXAGON   SQUARE   TRIANGLE

Figure 29 – Hexagon, square, triangle

Troubleshooting

Problem: The horse cannot or does not want to move the haunches to one side or the other.

Solution: From the ground, "in hand" the trainer should teach the horse to move the haunches. The trainer should stand left shoulder to left shoulder with the horse.

While holding the reins in the trainer's left hand, the trainer holds a dressage whip as if one were holding a sword and position the whip parallel to the ground at the level where a mounted rider's legs would be. The trainer, with one finger, lightly touches the horse's side where the rider's leg would be acting behind the girth, inviting the horse to displace his haunches away from him. If the horse does not respond, the trainer should lightly tap the horse on the thigh just above the hock until the horse has moved. When the horse has performed the intended response, the trainer should reward the horse with a gentle pat or caress his eyes to tell him that he did the right thing.

Repeating this action will eventually mobilize the haunches one step at a time. The trainer should repeat the same exercise at a slow and faster walk and, eventually, at the trot. When the horse has understood this well and is able and willing to displace his haunches, the trainer will ask a rider to sit on the horse's back. Still from the ground, the trainer will repeat all these exercises in the same manner. Little by little, the rider will replace the trainer and will be able to move the horse's haunches without any help from the ground. This simple progression should be executed over a period of a few days to allow the horse to truly assimilate this new exercise. A horse will always require patience and tact from the rider.

Figure 30 – Moving the haunches

• *Nota Bene* •

The rider should move her leg back one or two inches from the hip joint and NOT by bending the knee. When the rider is acting with a leg behind the girth, the rider's heel will move slightly up and down while the toe remains pointing upward. If the toe rises in the stirrup, besides revealing a lack of discretion in applying the aids, the rising will cause the rider's ankle and knee to lock interfering with the horse's hind leg on the same side as the active leg.

It might also be wise for the rider to wear a pair of spurs. If the horse picks up his legs and moves them forward in reaction to the whip, the horse will lift his legs more upward in reaction to the spurs, which is the desired action required to move the horse's haunches.

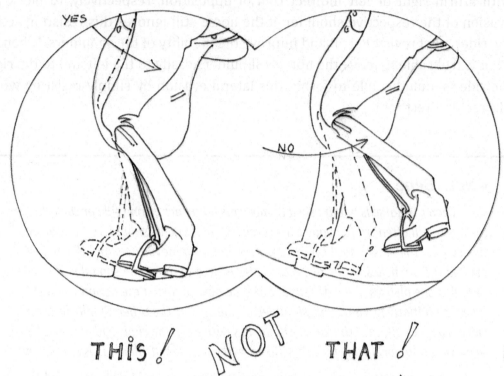

SLIDE THE LEG BACK FROM THE HIP ANGLE NOT BENDING AT THE KNEE

Figure 31 – This not That

Troubleshooting

Problem: The horse steps forward instead of moving his haunches.

Solution: The rider must immediately stop the horse by resisting with her back while simultaneously closing both hands on the reins. If the rider doubts the horse's obedience, she should revisit the transitions of walk-stop-walk, as discussed in Part A to make certain that the horse is well in front of her legs.

Problem: The horse wants to step backward.

63

Solution: The rider must make certain that she is not pulling on the reins. The rider must immediately act with both legs to keep the horse in place or to send him forward if he has stepped back. Revisiting part A will confirm the total obedience of the rider's legs.

Problem: The horse displaces his shoulders instead of his haunches.

Solution: If the horse moves the shoulders to the right or left, the rider must resist with a firm right or left indirect rein of opposition, respectively, to block any evasion of the respective shoulder. If the horse still ignores this resisting action, the rider must revisit Part B and improve the mobility of the shoulders. When the rider is truly able to move the horse's shoulders easily to the left and to the right, the rider should be able to forbid this lateral evasion by simply resisting with a discreet indirect rein.

• *Nota Bene* •

When the horse is being asked to move his haunches to one side or the other, the horse will often try to evade the exercise by moving his shoulders. To prevent this escape, the rider should first teach the horse to move the shoulders before moving the haunches. Logically, if the rider is able to move the shoulders in any direction she pleases, the rider should also be able to forbid the action when she takes the initiative to move his shoulder to one side or the other. Similarly, if the rider is able to displace the horse's haunches with ease, the rider will also be able to prevent or to forbid any initiative taken by the horse in displacing his haunches.

If, after a certain period of training time, the horse still does not bend his hocks, the trainer should try to ask for the rotation of the haunches around the shoulders while traveling uphill and downhill on a small incline. The horse then will be compelled to pick up his feet. When the horse is able to easily displace his haunches on either side, the rider will proceed in the same manner on the flat at a slow walk and very gradually at a more forward pace. This exercise should also be done at the trot following the same simple progression.

E.   Rein Back

The rein back is a two-beat gait in which the horse moves one diagonal biped at a time, i.e., left posterior with the right anterior followed by the right posterior with the left anterior. The rein back is an important exercise not to be neglected because it will further supple the horse's top line. When the horse is backing he must be calm, straight, and maintain his equilibrium. The horse should be moving backwards with two equal beats by the diagonal pairs, flexing his joints and lifting his legs.

How does the rider ask the horse to move backward?

1. Slow the walk almost to a stop.

2. Close both hands to interrupt the forward motion. To generate the backing motion, the rider must immediately and alternately open and close both hands on the reins while keeping both legs in contact with the horse's barrel. As the horse steps back the rider should incline her upper body very slightly forward to lighten the weight on the horse's back.

3. After the horse has performed the desired number of backward steps, the rider should lean backward slightly and send the horse forward by acting with both legs.

How does the rider teach the horse to move backward?

1. The rider should perform several walk-stop-walk transitions. When the horse is at the stop, the rider should allow the horse to stand a few seconds in total quietness.

2. From a stop, quietly ask the horse to alternately move his haunches one or two steps to one side and the other. Repeat this action a few times.

3. When the horse responds well in moving his haunches, the rider should send the horse forward, but immediately close both hands to interrupt the forward motion and then alternately act with each hand independently to generate the retrograde motion.

4. As soon as the horse has shown signs of understanding and steps backward with ease, the rider will slightly incline her upper body backward, act with both legs, and send the horse forward.

5. Gradually, over time, when the horse has learned the exercise, the rider will demand an increasing number of backward steps.

6. The horse should learn to step back from a stop, a walk, and later from a trot and eventually from the canter.

Troubleshooting

Problem: The horse cannot or refuses to step back.

Solution: The rider must practice moving the horse's haunches from a standing position until mobility becomes easy. Eliminating resistance by unlocking the hind legs is essential. If difficulty in backing persists, the rider will have to teach the horse to back "in hand" from the ground.

Figure 32 – Rein back

Problem: The horse does not back straight.

Solution: If the horse moves his haunches sideways as he steps back, rider should always correct the direction of the motion by replacing the shoulders in front of the hind legs. For example, if the horse's haunches are veering to the left, the rider will apply a right indirect rein to move the shoulders to the left to straighten the horse's body. Also, rotating the haunches around the shoulder several times (from left to right) will eventually eliminate this weakness. For instance, if the horse has a tendency to step back veering to the left due to a weaker left posterior or a stronger right posterior, the rider should practice pushing the haunches to the right several times applying the left leg behind the girth.

Problem: The horse drags his feet on the ground.

Solution: The rider can develop flexion by moving the horse's shoulders around the haunches and vice versa. If the horse persists in failing to lift his feet and bend his knees and hocks, the rider should demand the rein back traveling uphill and downhill on a slight incline.

• *Nota Bene* •

From a standing position, the rider can generate the rein back with the horse's right or left diagonal biped. For example, to invite the horse to begin backing with his right diagonal biped, the rider will act first with her right hand.

The rider must remember that the rein back is an exercise and should not be practiced as a chastisement when the horse does not obey.

F.   *Changing Directions*

Changing directions several times while gradually turning tighter will:

1. Develop the lateral flexibility of the horse's spinal column on each side (*ilio-spinal* muscles),

2. Supple the shoulders, especially the outside one (i.e., the right shoulder muscles will be extendedh while turning left; the left shoulder will gain suppleness while turning right)

3. Further engage the hind leg on the concave side and

4. Invite the other hind leg on the convex side to better propel.

With daily practice these turns will eventually become tighter. The rider should repeat the change of directions about five to seven consecutive times and gradually at closer intervals.

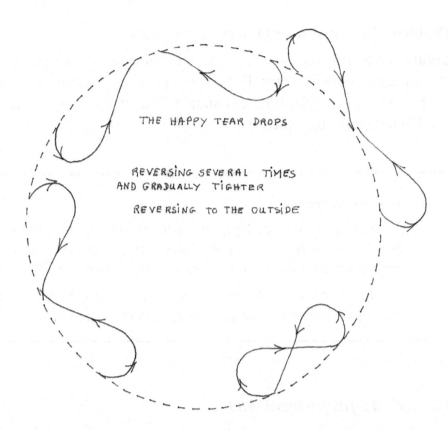

THE HAPPY TEAR DROPS

REVERSING SEVERAL TIMES
AND GRADUALLY TIGHTER

REVERSING TO THE OUTSIDE

Figure 33 – Changing directions

How does the rider change directions?

To change directions, the rider alternates using the inside right and left direct reins to change directions. In addition, the rider must:

1. The rider must look toward the direction of the motion.

2. Act with the inside direct rein and release the outside rein to allow the horse to turn his head in the new direction.

3. Move her outside hip forward while turning to keep the rider's hips parallel to the horse's shoulders. The rider's inside leg should act "at the girth," and carry more weight; the rider's outside leg will remain a little further back.

Troubleshooting

Problem: The horse cannot or does not want to turn to one side or the other.

Solution: At first the rider should not turn too tightly. Instead, the rider should try to discover what the horse is capable of doing on that particular day. Practicing daily, the rider should reduce the diameter of the half circle until, one day, the horse will be able to turn very tightly. To help the horse turn, the rider may raise her inside acting hand slightly to better bend the horse's neck. As soon as the horse has shown signs of obedience, the rider will lower her hand as a reward. Daily practice will improve the velocity of the turns. In cases of extreme resistance, the rider should revisit the zigzag training discussed in Part B of this progression.

Problem: The horse escapes the movement by swinging his haunches outside the turn.

Solution: The rider must be certain that she was not pulling on the active direct [inside] rein and should resist with the outside leg behind the girth. If the rider has not erred in applying the aids, she should revisit the training suggested in Part One, Section D.

Problem: The horse stops or slows down in the middle of the turn.

Solution: The rider must ask for a wider turn, soften the action of the active direct rein, and increase the action of the inside leg at the girth.

Problem: The horse trips while turning.

Solution: The more intense study of the lateral work should reduce and finally eliminate the stumbling.

The rider should work all of these basic exercises in both directions so that the horse becomes more symmetrical. Remember that after any lateral exercise, the horse must be asked to move straight and more forward until he makes this correction by himself.

• *Nota Bene* •

In turning, the rider must never pull on the acting direct rein because it will block the horse's inside shoulder and incite the horse's haunches to veer to the outside. While turning, the horse must remain as straight as possible.

The rider's inside leg at the girth will be the "active leg" if needed; the rider's outside leg will be a "position leg" to prevent the horse's haunches from drifting. Stated more simply: In turning to the right, the rider should act with a right direct rein, maintain her right leg at the girth and the left leg, the position leg, behind the girth and vice versa in turning to the left.

These exercises must be practiced daily in both directions until the horse has clearly understood and is able to perform them equally well in both directions. The rider must always use the same aids to gradually render him more receptive and available to the slightest demand and to avoid confusing the horse. To avoid muscle tetanization (cramping) caused by exaggerated practice, each exercise should be demanded only a few times per session in both directions. To rest, the horse while continuing the lessons, the rider should "go large" and travel on a straight line for awhile. The rider must remember that the horse must enjoy his work. Riders must always use her acquired knowledge and study how to correctly perform each movement demanded of the horse.

When practicing these exercises, the horse will show all his strong attributes as well as his weaknesses. In training the horse, if the rider encounters more difficulty while working one side of the horse, the problem, very often, is due to a weakness in the opposite side. For example, if the horse has difficulty in moving his shoulders to the left, the cause of this weakness could likely stem from a stiffness in the right shoulder. To remedy the weakness, it would be best to do more work on the horse's easy side and temporarily forgo work on the horse's weaker side. When the horse is very comfortable and can perform the work well on his stronger side, the opposite weaker side will no longer pose as much difficulty as the horse will have developed greater strength on this weaker side as well.

Plate 3 – Gala uniform of the Colonel, Écuyer en Chef of the Cadre Noir of Saumur

LESSON TWO

The Working Phase, Beginning of Dressage, also called "Low School Dressage"

The Trot

At the trot, a two-beat gait, the horse jumps from one diagonal biped to the other, i.e., right posterior with left anterior followed by the left posterior with the right anterior. The speed is approximately nine miles per hour.

Lesson Two will be the working phase for the horse. The exercises will be the same as those practiced in Lesson One, except that the exercises will be performed at the trot. Working at the trot is fundamental to perfecting the horse's suppleness and enable the horse to perfect his natural agility. The work will be performed on a figure eight pattern of two tangent circles of 20 meters in diameter.

Remember: To develop the symmetry of the horse's muscle system, all exercises must always be repeated in the other direction.

Before beginning the exercises of these lessons, the rider should trot the horse for a few minutes as a warm up to ready the horse to begin work at the trot as well as to allow the rider to check her horse's balance and straightness. While trotting the horse, the rider should try to maintain the same tempo, using her hands to act as "side reins" to remind the horse to respect the bit. A less experienced rider should rest her hands on the horse's neck while maintaining an active forward motion with her legs from time to time or only when necessary.

Nota Bene

To teach the horse to accept and respect the bit, "side reins" or Lauffer reins were allegedly developed by the German Military. Side reins are considered a fixed piece of equipment. The side reins consist of two leather straps that are attached from the bit to the girth, positioned below the saddle flaps. Adjusted properly, the side reins should be used ONLY when the horse is trotting because the horse's head and neck are not moving. The walk and the canter have too much of a pendulum action and the side reins will cause the bit to hit the horse's mouth, inciting the horse to withdraw his head behind the vertical.

When practicing these exercises, the rider may encounter problems due to the horse's misunderstanding or from the horse's inability to execute the movement properly. It is always wise to return to Part One and improve the study at the walk. In equitation, patience and repetition are very important considerations to properly train a horse and to avoid causing the horse stress. The quality of the work at the trot is the culmination of the real understanding of the work at the walk, a proof of nine, so to speak.

A. Longitudinal Exercise: Transitions Trot-Walk-Trot

Transitions from the trot to the walk and back to the trot will develop and further improve the horse's obedience to the rider's aids and enhance the engagement of the horse's hindquarters. At first, the transition will be demanded at each cardinal point.

Figure 34 – Cardinal points

73

Troubleshooting

Problem: The horse does not want to trot.

Solution: In case of lack of obedience to the rider's leg command, the rider must immediately re-enforce the demand by either acting firmly with both legs or apply the whip on the horse's shoulder to induce the forward motion. Revisiting Lesson One may also be wise. A horse must be in front of the legs, meaning that the horse must be ready to respond instantaneously to the rider's slightest demand.

Problem: The horse does not want to walk.

Solution: If the horse does not respond after closing and opening the fingers a couple of times, the rider should shorten the reins, rotate both the wrists to turn her palms face up and slowly elevate simultaneously both hands in a vertical plane until the horse has returned to the walk. In time and with practice, less hand elevation will be required, until, one day, the horse will respond to a very light hand action. But, the rider must always keep this idea of elevating of the hands in mind as a secret weapon in her arsenal of training tools.

Problem: The horse does not really walk to create the transitions.

Solution: If the horse is not walking calmly, the rider has a few options:

1. The rider can stop the horse and give him some time to relax.
2. The rider can ask the horse to zigzag several times, pushing his shoulders to the left and right.
3. Interrupt the work and give the horse a well-deserved break.

B. Lateral Exercise: Zigzags

Zigzags will laterally bend the horse's top line and develop agility of the horse's shoulders.

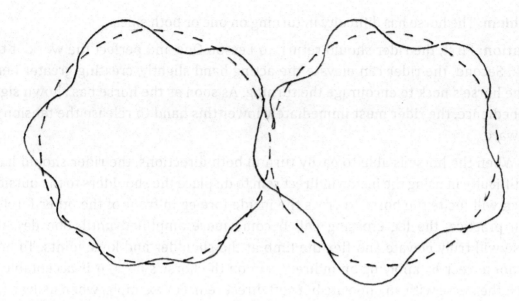

Figure 35 – Zigzag

Figure 36 – Loops left indirect rein

Problem: The horse has difficulty in turning on one or both sides.

Solution: First, the rider should return to Lesson One and perfect the work at the walk. Second, the rider can elevate the acting hand slightly, creating greater bend in the horse's neck to encourage the turning. As soon as the horse has shown signs of obedience, the rider must immediately lower this hand to release the tension as a reward.

When the horse is able to easily turn in both directions, the rider should have no difficulty in using the inside indirect rein to displace the shoulders to the outside, which will incite the horse to cross the inside foreleg in front of the other foreleg. With practice, the leg crossing will become more amplified until, one day, the horse will truly elevate and flex the limb at the shoulder and knee joints. To help the horse veer by applying an indirect rein on the horse's neck, it is acceptable to assist the horse with an opposite but soft direct rein. For example, when using a left indirect rein to push the horse's shoulders to the right, the rider may help, in case of difficulties, by simultaneously acting with the right direct rein to lead the horse toward the desired direction.

Figure 37 – Indirect rein

C. Longitudinal Exercise: Lengthening and Shortening the Strides at the Trot

Lengthening and shortening the strides at the trot will longitudinally flex the horse's top line and improve engagement and power of the hind legs.

Problem: The horse cannot or will not slow the trot.

Solution: Improving the lengthening the shortening at the walk would be a good start. Next, the rider should emphasize perfecting the downward transition when practicing alternating the trotting and walking gaits. When the rider is successful in the transition from the trot to the walk, the rider should also be able to reduce the speed of the trot because to be able to walk from the trot, the horse will first slow the pace. Et voila! The rest is merely a question of practice.

For example, trotting on the reference figure eight, the rider will divide this figure into four equal halves. Each of these halves will be divided into three equal parts. At the trot, as the rider enters the first half, she will demand a gradual augmentation in speed three times in this segment. When the rider enters the second half of the reference figure eight she will gradually reduce the speed of this segment three times. For the next half circle the rider will repeat the gradual augmentation of speed as she did in the first part of the figure eight. After several sessions, the horse will understand what to do and either will obey more promptly or anticipate the demand.

At the rising trot, as our British friends would say, to slow the speed, the rider should resist with her back muscles and several time simultaneously close and open the outside hand. When trotting, tracking to the right, the rider's left hand will be acting by closing and opening the fingers several times. To be more precise, the rider should close the left hand when the horse's left shoulder is moving backward and open the same hand when the shoulder is moving forward again. When the horse's shoulder is moving backward it means that the corresponding foot below is in contact with the ground. If the rider, at this particular moment, closes her hand, she will oblige that foot to stay on the ground a little longer, which, as a result, will slow the pace. Also, to lengthen the horse's stride, it is always better for the rider to squeeze both legs for the duration of 3 or 4 strides instead of repeatedly squeezing and releasing her legs at every stride.

D. Lateral Exercise: Moving the Haunches

Moving the haunches will laterally develop the flexion of the hind legs to increase power of the stifle muscles.

Problem: The horse has a difficulty in moving his haunches laterally.

Solution: Return to Lesson One and improve the exercise at the walk. Then, on the reference circle, the rider should ask the horse to move his haunches to the outside of the circumference for only one or two strides. As the horse becomes better able to move his haunches, the rider can gradually ask the horse to move his haunches an additional stride. The rider must be attentive to the horse's reaction and make certain that too much is not demanded of the horse. Overdoing the exercise or the rider being too ardent in her demands will be counter-productive.

Figure 38 – Moving the haunches

• Nota Bene •

Practiced daily, these exercises will transform the horse's body and mental attitude in a rather short period of time. They also will uncover the horse's strengths and weaknesses.

LESSON THREE

Further Study

The Canter

The canter appears as a mixture of the walk and trot. The canter is a four-phase gait in which the horse's three successive beats are followed by a suspension phase where all four feet are off the ground. The horse can travel at the canter on either the left or right lead. When the horse is traveling on the left lead, the horse's left lateral biped, i.e., the left front and left hind, reaches further forward than the right; at the right lead canter, the right lateral biped, i.e., the right front and the right hind, reaches further forward than the left. At the canter the horse travels approximately twelve miles per hour.

At the canter, the order of the footfalls for the right lead are indicated as follows:

1. Left posterior

2. Left diagonal, i.e., left anterior and right posterior

3. Right anterior

4. Suspension phase when all four hooves are off the ground

It will be the opposite for the left lead canter.

Because it is difficult for one to perceive the synchronization of the horse's legs at the canter, artists have made some interesting renderings of the horse at the canter in old paintings and lithographs. In the 19th century, with the invention of cinematography and the origin of slow motion by the Lumière Brothers, August and Louis, one could easily see how the horse moves his legs and determine the horse's footfall at the canter.

Before studying the canter work, the rider should educate her horse to promptly respond to the aids and obtain perfect transitions. The rider must first teach canter departures from the trot, then the walk and finally from the halt and even the rein back. The rider also must master the downward transitions from the canter. The rider's aids must be clearly and perfectly understood to allow the horse to basically execute the transitions with very little solicitations from the rider. The canter departures on the right lead, for instance, should be achieved by allowing the horse's right diagonal biped, (i.e., right anterior leg and left posterior leg) to reach ahead of the left diagonal.

Following are different techniques and aids to ask for a right lead canter on the reference circle.

1. To decrease the amplification of the horse's left shoulder, the rider should resist by acting with a left "direct rein of opposition" to slow the left anterior leg and allow the right anterior leg to lead.

2. To place the horse's right shoulder ahead of the left, the rider should act with a right "indirect rein" to shift the horse's weight to his left shoulder thereby slowing the pace and allowing the horse's right anterior leg to lead.

3. To lower the horse's left hip, the rider should act with her left leg "behind the girth" combined with a left "direct rein of opposition". This action will deviate the horse's haunches to the right and incite left hip to lower and better engage the left posterior leg.

4. To raise the horse's right hip, the rider should act with her right leg "at the girth" to incite the horse to lift his right hip and increase the engagement of the right posterior leg.

The rider's aids should be the opposite for the left lead.

Riding Masters have established three classical ways to generate the right lead canter depart:

1. Acting with the left lateral aids, i.e., The left direct rein of opposition and the left leg slightly behind the girth. Comte d'Aure. (1799 - 1863). *Figure 39*

2. Acting with the right diagonal aids, i.e. ,The right indirect rein and the left leg slightly behind the girth. James Fillis (1834 - 1913). *Figure 40*

3. Acting with the right lateral aids, i.e., The right indirect rein and the right leg at the girth. François Baucher (1796 - 1873). *Figure 41*

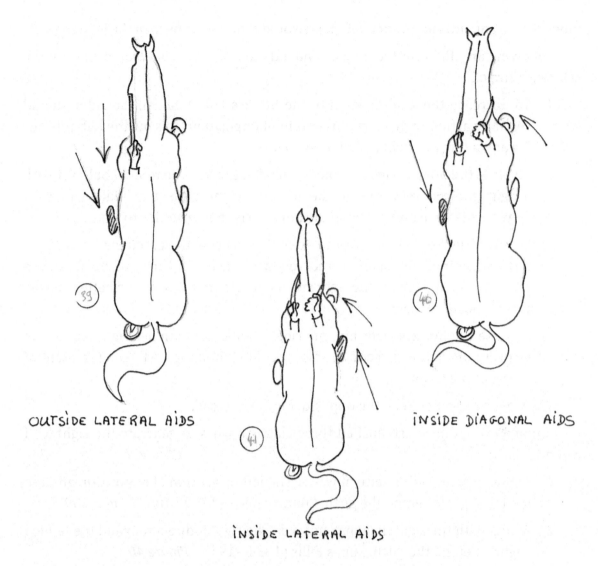

OUTSIDE LATERAL AIDS

INSIDE DIAGONAL AIDS

INSIDE LATERAL AIDS

(l - r) Figure 39, Figure 41, Figure 40 – Three Canter Departs

Once the canter aids are placed, the rider can demand the departure by acting simultaneously with either both legs or with one predominant leg. The promptness of the horse's obedience will depend on the horse's level of education and the rider's timing. For best results ,the rider should ask for the right canter depart with her legs when the horse's left shoulder is moving backward.

Progression to generate the right lead canter by applying the outside lateral aids.

The rider should begin at a rising trot on the reference circle tracking right on the outside diagonal biped.

A. When the rider has reached the prior decided point on the reference circle, the rider should switch to rise to the right diagonal biped (inside) to further engage the left posterior leg.
B. After trotting a few strides on the right diagonal biped, the rider should simultaneously apply the outside lateral aids; left indirect rein of opposition and left leg behind the girth,
C. The rider should ask the horse for an increase of speed until he falls into a canter. On a circle to the right, the horse should generate the correct right canter lead.
D. After one revolution at the canter, the rider should come back to a brief trot and then return to the walk.

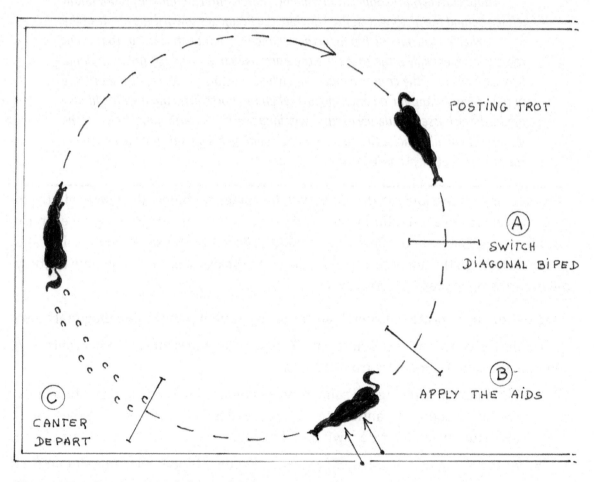

Figure 42 – Canter outside lateral aids

Rehearsing this progression and always asking for a canter depart in the same manner and at the same decided place on the circle will rapidly instill a prompt response from the horse.

This progression has the advantage of inviting the horse to choose the proper canter lead. The rider creates an unbalance on purpose by placing the horse's nose to the outside of the circle and bringing the haunches toward the inside. The rider, by increasing the speed until the horse can no longer trot, causes the horse to automatically fall into the canter on the proper lead.

• *Nota Bene* •

The left direct rein of opposition will slow the left anterior and the predominant left leg behind the girth will slightly deviate the haunches toward the inside of the circle, lowering the outside hip to further engage the left posterior leg. To prevent too much excess speed the first time the horse is being asked to canter, it would be wise to ask for the canter depart only when the horse is facing the short side of the arena. Asking for a canter depart when the horse is facing a wall will also diminish the horse's tendency to run. Switching to the inside diagonal biped at the rising trot will also incite the horse to better engage his outside hind leg allowing the horse to better prepare for the canter departure.

After several sessions, as the rider switches diagonal biped, the horse will try to steal the canter depart. It simply means that the horse has understood the exercise but his timing is a little off. The rider should proceed in the same manner but at a sitting trot. When the horse properly responds to the exercise, it will be time to study the progression in Step 2 that follows.

Progression to generate the right lead canter by applying the inside diagonal aids

On the reference circle, the rider should begin from the rising trot and progress to generate the canter departure from the walk.

A. The rider by applying the same progression used for the outside lateral aids, the horse soon will anticipate the rider's demand and try steal the canter departure when the rider switches diagonal.

B. At the rising trot, instead of switching diagonal biped, the rider should first reduce the trotting speed, lightly sit in the saddle and simultaneously apply the right diagonal aids, i.e., right indirect rein and left leg behind the girth.

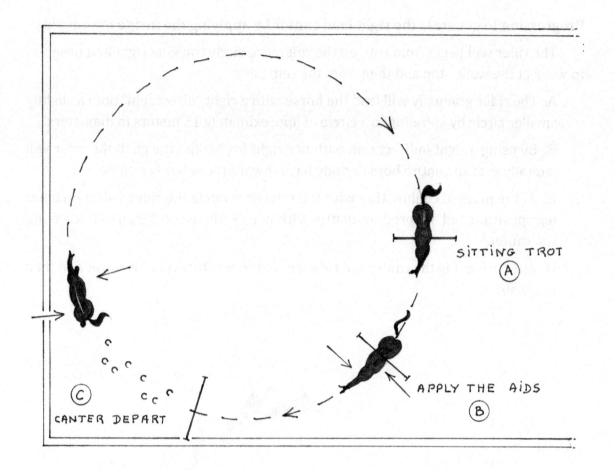

Figure 43 – Diagonal aids

This progression has the advantage of maintaining the horse's in his natural balance at the canter by holding his nose and haunches on the same side as the lead. Being bent in this position, the horse will automatically leap into the canter on the proper lead either from the trot or the walk.

• Nota Bene •

The right indirect rein will burden the left anterior leg to slow it down, free the action of the right front; a predominant left leg behind the girth will slightly deviate the haunches toward the inside of the circle and lower the left hip to further engage the left posterior leg. The sitting trot should help to reduce the speed.

Progression to generate the right lead canter by applying the inside lateral aids

The rider will begin from trot, on the reference circle tracking right and progress to work at the walk, stop and then from the rein back.

A. The rider gradually will lead the horse with a right "direct rein" onto a slightly smaller circle by spiraling to a circle of approximately 15 meters in diameters.

B. By using a right indirect rein with her right leg behind the girth the rider will laterally veer the entire horse's body back toward the reference circle.

C. At the place of conjunction with the reference circle the rider will switch her legs position and act predominantly with her inside leg at the girth to demand the canter.

D. After achieving the canter the rider should return to a very brief trot and then to a walk.

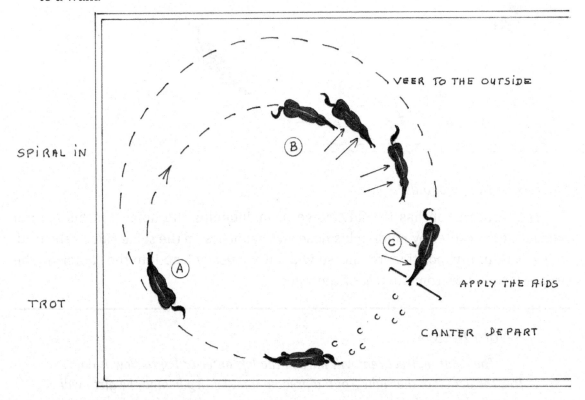

Figure 44 – Inside lateral aids

This progression has the advantage of maintaining the horse's nose on the same side as the lead while his haunches remains in line with his fore hand. This method is preferred because the horse's body stays straight and in perfect equilibrium, ready for the advanced levels.

Troubleshooting

Problem: The horse does not give a canter depart.

Solution: The obedience to the rider's legs should be supported immediately by a decisive action with the whip on the horse's left (outside) shoulder to stimulate and create an instantaneous reaction from the horse.

Problem: The horse increase the speed at the trot and does not change gait.

Solution: The rider should revisit the trot-walk-trot transitions as well of the lengthening and shortening at walk and trot, especially insisting on the downward transitions to better control the horse's evasion.

Problem: The horse takes the wrong lead.

Solution: The rider may have wrongly applied the aids. Practicing this exercise should teach both horse and rider to become accurate. If the horse persist taking the wrong lead, the rider's first reaction should not be to punish the horse by brutally stopping him. Instead the rider should maintain the incorrect lead and guide or lead the horse onto a smaller circle while still sustaining the incorrect canter lead. After cantering in this uncomfortable mode for several rotations, the horse will either switch canter lead or break to a trot. If the latter occurs, the rider will immediately demand for a canter departure again. When the horse is on the proper lead the rider should go "large", i.e., leave the small circle and go straight, and reward the horse with a gentle pat on the neck before or after bringing him back to the walk. After several trials the horse will begin taking the correct lead without any confusion.

The horse should not learn that if he makes an error, the rider will automatically bring him back to the walk. Often when the horse makes a mistake, the rider should maintain the incorrect mode to show the horse how uncomfortable it is. While horses lack common sense, they are not unintelligent.

The horse may also have a physical handicap. Nevertheless, before asking a Veterinarian to evaluate the problem, the rider might save money by reviewing the Lesson One, Part One and insist on better mobility from the horse's front and back legs in both directions at the walk and trot. By reworking the horse's body, the problem should resolved itself.

• *Nota Bene* •

It is particularly important that the horse not learn that taking the wrong lead or cross cantering is a punishable fault as the rider may encounter greater difficulties in the advance stage of the horse's training when trying to obtain flying changes of lead.

Problem: The horse canters on the forehand.

Solution: The horse will canter on his forehand when his balance in impeded. Continued work in lengthening and shortening the strides, zigzagging, canter-rein back-canter transitions, working on circles with the haunches inside and gradually working smaller circles will progressively improve the horse's insufficient balance.

Problem: The horse canters too fast.

Solution: The progression to resolve this problem is as follows:

1. The rider should review the transitions changing gaits.

2. The rider should determine which speed the horse prefers.

3. While cantering, the rider should increase the horse's preferred speed for about 10 to 20 strides to temper the horse's desire to remain in his comfort zone.

4. The rider should then slow this increase of speed to the horse's preferred pace.

5. Each session the rider should repeat the same exercise but increase the speed less and gradually decrease the pace more. With repetition, time, and patience, eventually the horse will canter at the speed desired by the rider.

• *Nota Bene* •

For the first lessons the rider should avoid maintaining the canter for too long a period. After several sessions, the rider should gradually increase the time spent at the canter until one day the horse is able to maintain the gait on his own for a long time with minimal efforts. Then and only then should the study at the canter will really begin.

Progression to obtain the right lead canter from the walk.

On the reference circle tracking the right at the trot:

1. The rider should gradually lead the horse onto a smaller circle of about 15 meters in diameter. With a right indirect rein and a right leg behind the girth the rider will move the horse sideways back toward the reference circle. As the horse reaches the reference circle the rider should gradually slow the trot before asking for a canter departure.

Important: When the horse reaches the reference circle his shoulders should be slightly leading. If the haunches were leading, it may solicit the wrong lead.

2. As the horse, moving sideways, reaches the reference circle, the rider should slow the trot to almost the speed of the walk before asking for a canter departure.

3. As the horse, moving sideways, reaches the reference circle, the rider should ask for one walking stride before demanding a canter departure.

4. As the horse, moving sideways, reaches the reference circle, the rider should ask for two or three walking strides prior to the canter departure.

The rider should continues gradually asking for more walking strides until the horse becomes very obedient to the canter departure from the walk. At this point the rider should not need the preparatory portion of the reference circle and may ask for the canter at any time and from anywhere. To teach the horse to canter from a stop the progression will be similar. From the trot or a walk, the rider should stop for a brief moment and demand a canter departure. Next the rider would stop for a second or two longer. Gradually , the rider should require the horse to stand longer before demanding the next canter departure. The progression for the left lead canter will be the same.

For the future work at the canter such as counter-canter and flying changes of lead, it will be mandatory that the horse give perfect canter departures on either lead from the walk and the stop. The scientific study shows that a horse, to generate a canter departure from the walk, always should always begin the transition by propelling his body with his hind legs. When trotting however the horse will use his front legs which will create a problem when studying the changes of lead at the canter.

Troubleshooting

Problem: The horse does not slow the trot before the canter departure.

Solution: The rider must revisit Lesson One Part One and reconfirm the obedience to the rider's legs and hands by practicing the downward transitions and by lengthening and shortening the strides at the walk, trot and canter.

Problem: The horse anticipates the canter depart.

Solution: Anticipation is not necessarily undesirable. It simply means that the horse has understood the demands but his timing is inaccurate. The rider's patience will be tested. In case of too much nervousness, the rider should interrupt the work for a few minutes or simply postpone it to the next session.

Progression for the downward transition from the canter to the walk.

On the reference circle, tracking right:

The rider should ask for the trot before the walk. The rider must determine how many comfortable trotting strides the horse may need to rebalance himself before walking. Then, the rider, may establish a program to teach the horse to immediately walk from the canter.

For example:

1. After the canter, trot the horse for 7 strides before asking for the walk. Practice this exercise for 2 consecutive weeks until the transition becomes absolutely easy.
2. After the canter, trot the horse for 6 strides before asking for the walk. Rehearse this exercise for 2 weeks again.
3. After the canter, trot the horse for 5 strides before asking for the walk. Review this exercise for another two weeks.

Every two weeks, the rider reduces the trotting strides by one stride until she has reached the moment when, effortlessly, she can ask directly for the walk. This method, if not rushed, should enable the rider to obtain the transition canter-walk transition without difficulty. They are other methods to accomplish this task but for a less experience rider or a difficult horse, this will be an easy progression to obtain successful results within a rather short period of time.

Before working the canter the rider should confirm all the upward and downward transitions and make certain that the horse is able to maintain the canter for a progressively longer period.

PROGRESSIVELY CANTER LONGER, LONGER AND LONGER

Figure 45 – Canter longer

The basic canter education, including all upward and downward transitions already inculcated in the horse, should greatly facilitate the canter work-study. Often the basic exercises will be similar to the work performed at the walk and trot with some minors variations because the horse walks one way, trots one way but canters in two ways: on the left lead or the right lead.

To teach the horse to maintain the canter by himself, to be "on automatic pilot" so to speak, the rider while cantering, should avoid doing anything except confirm her proper position: sitting upright, maintaining her aids in place especially her inside leg at the girth and outside leg behind the girth. The rider should remain totally quiet and even passive allowing the horse to carry her. To maintain a constant tempo, the rider should count in her mind repeatedly in sets from one to ten. If at any time, the horse alters the speed or changes the gait he will disrupt the counting and the rider should automatically and immediately apply the necessary corrections to preserve or re-establish the counting and the canter.

• Nota Bene •

If the rider decides to canter 50 strides, instead of consecutively counting from 1 to 50, she should count five sets of ten strides beginning each set with its number, i.e., 1,2,3,...10; 2, 2, 3,.....10; through 5, 2, 3, 4, 5.... 10, which will allow the rider to remember how many sets of ten strides she has ridden.

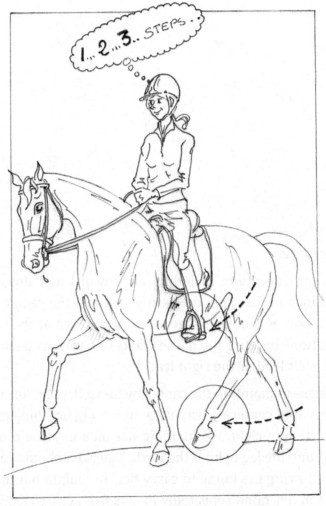

Figure 46 – Activity of the posterior

Phase One. Steady the Pace.

To maintain the same speed at the canter, the rider should begin the practice as follows:

1. On a 20 meters reference circle, with a line drawn to mark the beginning and the end of the circle, the rider should count the number of strides the horse canters within one complete revolution. If the rider has maintained the same tempo at the canter, she would count an average of 22 to 24 strides.

2. The rider should ride two consecutive circles with the objective to obtain the exact same number of strides for each revolution. Practice will help in reaching this goal.

3. The rider should repeat the above exercise, except she should canter the same number of strides for another revolution.

4. The rider should continue in the same manner and gradually increase the number of revolutions while maintaining the same tempo and counting the exact same number of strides. Continued practice will allow the rider and the horse to maintain a steady tempo.

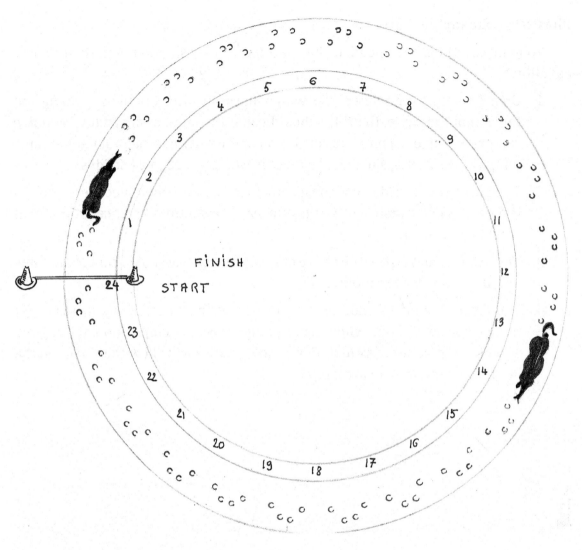

Figure 47 – 24 strides

Phase Two. Shorten the Canter Strides.

1. On the same reference circle the rider should now add 2 strides to her original counting, i.e., instead of cantering 24 strides the horse will canter now 26 strides. To fit these additional strides within the same reference circle, the rider must slow and shorten the canter strides.

2. The rider should continue practicing in the same manner for two, three, four or more revolutions.

Phase Three. Lengthening the Canter Strides.

1. On the same reference circle the rider should now reduce the number of canter strides by two. To accomplish cantering 22 strides within the same circumference, the rider must lengthen the horse's canter strides.

2. The rider should repeat the exercise by increasing the number of revolutions while maintaining the same tempo.

Exercises to Improve the Canter

A.   Gait Transitions

To improve the horse's balance and cadence at the canter, the rider should practice canter-trot-canter transitions or even better, canter-walk-canter, canter-stop-canter transitions. The rider's aids should be the same as any transitions walk- trot-walk and walk-stop-walk except that the rider may slightly act more with the hand associated with the canter lead, (right hand for the right lead and vice versa) to better stop the lead.

B.   Moving the Shoulders

Because the horse has been already educated to respond to the direct and indirect rein, the rider should be able to move the horse's shoulders in either directions. If the rider encounter any difficulties , she should revisit Lesson One, Part One.

C.   Lengthen and Shorten the Canter.

The rider's aids should be the same as those used in lengthening and shortening the strides at the trot and walk, except that she may emphasize the action with her active leg at the girth to lengthen the stride. To shorten the rider should resist with her back while simultaneously acting with her left hand so that she does not disrupt the right lead.

D.   Moving the Haunches at the Canter.

Because the horse can canter on either the right or left lead, moving the haunches should be done only toward the working lead, i.e., to the right for the right lead and to the left for the left lead. Asking the horse to move the haunches to the opposite side of the lead may dissociate the horse's foot falls and disunite the canter and result in the horse "cross-cantering" (cross-cantering is when the horse simultaneously canters on the right lead with the forelegs and canters on the left lead with the hind legs or vice versa). Disuniting his hind legs will generate an unbalance so that the horse, to prevent from falling, will instinctively break to a trot or swap canter lead.

• *Nota Bene* •

In earlier centuries riders allowed their horses to canter slightly sideways to maintain their natural mode of traveling. Flying changes of lead were rarely performed, and certainly, were not codified. In the mid-XIX century, François Baucher demonstrated that horses could easily change lead and furthered his discovery of the " tac au tac " (tempi flying changes of lead at every strides). The key to success, explained François Baucher, was not to allow a horse to canter sideways but maintain his body absolutely STRAIGHT.

Today, riders consider cross-cantering a sign of a disunited gait. But who is to say? As François Baucher showed for the flying change, one day, someone may discover whether there are merits to cross-cantering...

Counter-canter

The horse is said to be at the counter-canter when he is cantering on the right lead while tracking left or on the left lead tracking right.

The advantages of the counter-canter study are listed below.

- To confirm the stability and the tempo of the canter on both leads,
- To confirm the horizontal balance, i.e. equal weight distribution among the four legs.
- To straighten the horse who has a tendency to canter sideways, i,e haunches deviating toward the lead direction.
- To amplify the canter strides (an opposite bend to the canter lead amplifies the stride).
- To flex the horse's loins, which will result in activating and engaging the horse's hind legs.

Rider's aids for the counter-canter are the same as the correct canter leads but in reverse: Tracking to the left the aids for the right lead canter will be as follows (it will be the opposite for the left lead):

- Right active indirect rein;

- Left passive rein to allow the action of the right rein;

- Right active leg at the girth;

- Left passive leg behind the girth;

- The rider, sitting straight and centered, with slightly more weight on the left seat bone, if necessary.

• *Nota Bene* •

If the horse is inexperienced, the rider should support and maintain the lead with her legs. When the horse is confirmed and more capable in maintaining the counter-canter, the rider will act tactfully with the leg at the girth and only when necessary.

How to prepare the horse for the counter-canter.

1. At the trot follow the patterns of "counter changes" with gradually smaller angles. (Counter changes are two oblique lines going in opposite directions.) To become more flexible, the horse must learn to change direction with ease.

2. At the canter follow the same progression as the preparatory trot work,

3. From the correct canter lead, reverse direction and maintain the counter-canter on a straight line and follow the track of the arena.

4. Maintain the horse at the counter-canter on a circle, and with practice gradually maintain the counter-canter on smaller circles.

5. Maintain the counter-canter while riding a figure eight,

6. Maintain the counter-canter on a serpentine.

7. Teach the horse to begin the counter-canter from the opposite direction, i.e., begin with the right lead while traveling left.

Figure 48 – The classroom

• Nota Bene •

To avoid difficulties when studying the counter-canter, the rider should always look in the direction that she is going, which will place her body in the correct position and support the canter lead with her leg acting at the girth.

If a horse has a poor balance at the canter, the counter-canter should be taught as soon as the horse is able to maintain the canter on both leads. If the horse has a good balance, the counter-canter will be less necessary and should be taught after the horse has learned the flying changes of lead.

Troubleshooting

Problem: The horse cannot maintain the counter-canter lead in either one or the other direction or both.

Solution:

1. The rider should maintain fixity and steadiness of her aids because when the horse is not confirmed, the rider's slightest unnecessary movement may disrupt the horse's equilibrium causing him to change lead or break to a trot on his weak side.

2. The rider should need to re-visit the rotation of the shoulders around the haunches and the rotation of the haunches around the shoulders. These rotations will supple the horse laterally and remedy any weakness.

The rider should also work on a larger counter change angle. Time and practice will allow both horse and rider to become more familiar with the aids and the turns. When the horse is more agile, the horse should be able to maintain the counter-canter in either directions.

• *Nota Bene* •

To improve the jump and the amplification of the canter strides when the horse is confirmed in performing the counter-canter, the rider should place the horse's head in a counter bend, (to the left for the right lead and vice-versa to the left lead). Then solicit the horse to lower his neck and head before demanding for an increase of the speed.

The counter-canter is also a wonderful test for the rider to determine her fixity in the saddle, i.e., the absence of all unnecessary body movement.

LESSON FOUR

Exercises

These exercises should be performed following the pattern of a large figure eight.

A. Transitions changing gaits;

B. Zigzags, moving the shoulders;

C. Lengthening and shortening the gaits;

D. Moving the haunches.

Now that the rider has some of the basics exercises at hand, she should apply them following the pattern of a reference figure eight (two tangent circles of 20 meters in diameter). The goals in reviewing each exercises in both directions, inside and outside, to perfect the horse's obedience, symmetry, activity, suppleness and balance.

Exercise One.   Transitions, Changing Gaits

At each cardinal point North, East, South and West, or locations decided earlier, the rider should first demand trot-walk-trot transitions. Then to confirm the obedience to the rider's aids and the ability to engage and push with the hind legs, the rider should demand trot-walk-stop-walk-trot transitions. When the horse becomes more receptive, the rider should demand transitions trot-stop-trot.

Troubleshooting

Problem: The horse has difficulty for the trot-stop-trot transitions.

Solution: Once the horse can easily switch from walk-stop-walk and trot-walk-trot it should be only a matter of time and practice before he is able to blend the two exercises into one to obtain trot-stop-trot. An easy progression method is as follows:

1. Ask for a transition from the trot to the stop allowing the horse to walk three or four steps before stopping, and walk three or four before trotting.

2. Gradually over a period of time the rider should reduce the walking steps to two, then to one and finally none.

Figure 49 – Trot walk stop

Exercise Two.   Zigzags

At the walk and at the trot, acting only with the right direct and then a right indirect rein, the rider should follow the undulations of the winding path of a serpentine (slalom), first tracking right and then tracking left. It is understood that when the rider changes circle the action of the right hand should remain, i.e., right direct and right indirect rein.

• *Nota Bene* •

Acting with the right hand tracking both to the right and to the left will prove that the horse is able to displace his shoulders in both directions with ease. The rider, tracking right should be pushing the horse's shoulders to the outside (left) but while tracking left she should be soliciting the horse to move his shoulders to the inside (also left) which is somewhat more challenging for both horse and rider. Accomplishing this exercise will clearly show to that the horse has perfectly understood the rider's demand and is fully able to perform the exercises well in both directions. If the horse has difficulties bringing his shoulders toward the inside of the second circle, it will clearly indicate that the rider must, without question re-visiting Lesson One, Part One. When the horse is confirmed with both indirect reins (right and left), the rider may ask the horse to slalom using indirect reins only i.e., alternately pushing the shoulders to the right with the left indirect rein and then to the left with the right indirect rein. It should also be time to ask for the same exercises traveling on a straight line.

Figure 50 – Zigzag on straight line

Exercise Three.   Lengthening and Shortening the Gaits

Every half of the reference circles of the figure eight, at both the walk and trot, the rider should demand either an increase or a decrease in speed. For instance: for the first half circle the rider should progressively demand a more forward walk; as the horse reaches the second half the rider should reduce that speed; Then the next half circle, the rider should again accelerate gait, etc. It will be the same for the trot, the rider should lengthen and shorten every half circle.

This exercise should also be demanded while traveling on a straight line: lengthening the strides on the long side of the arena, and shortening the strides on the short sides or vice versa.

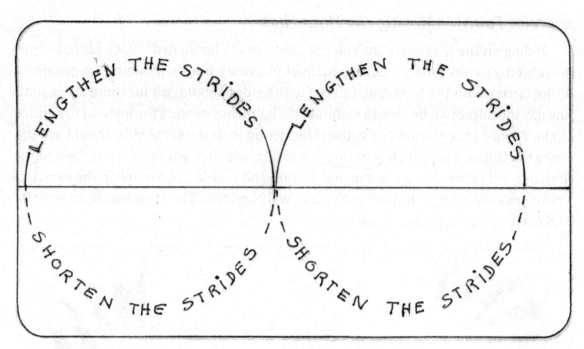

Figure 51 – Lengthen shorten

Troubleshooting

Problem: The horse has difficulty in truly lengthening the stride and opening the gaits.

Solution: It will be logical to first ask for very little increase or decrease in speed. For example: the rider may divide each half circle into three equal portions and at each juncture demand a little more variations in speed. Over time the horse will know the exercise and respond with more satisfaction.

• *Nota Bene* •

While lengthening the trot, the horse will gain in length what he loses in height, which in the upper levels will develop into a "medium trot" and even an "extended trot." While shortening the trot, the horse will gain in height what he loses in length, which later will become a "School trot" (similar to the low Passage).

Exercise Four.   Moving the Haunches

Riding on the first circle the rider should ask the horse to displace his haunches outside only two or three steps several times in a row while maintaining the geometry of the circles with the forehand. Gradually the rider should ask for more steps until one day the horse will be able to maintain his haunches outside throughout the entire circle. Then, on the second circle, the rider, acting with the same aids, should ask the horse to displace his haunches toward the inside, which might be more challenging at first, but will prove that the horse understood and is able to accomplish the exercise. This work should be performed both at the walk and trot. The same exercises must be practiced on a straight line as well.

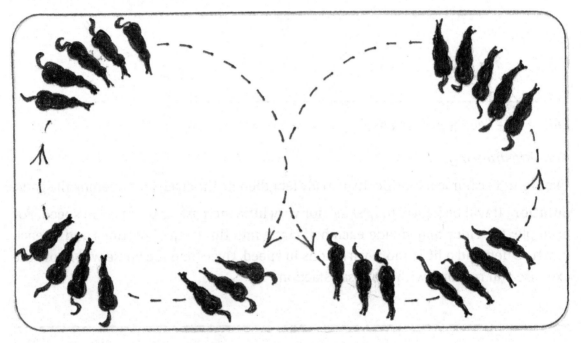

Figure 52 – Haunches in and out work on a figure 8

Troubleshooting

Problem: The horse has greater difficulty displacing his haunches to one side than the other.

Solution: Working the easy side at first will greatly facilitate the progression of the training. When the easy side improves, working the horse's less flexible side should be less problematic because the horse will respond by a conditioned reflex. When the rider feels that one side is stiffer than the other, the problem usually lies on the opposite side. For example a poor sideways motion of the right hind leg will most likely stem from a stiffness of the left hind leg or vice-versa.

• Nota Bene •

Horses, just like people, are not congenitally symmetrical. One goal of these progressions is to reduce the natural asymmetries of the horse so that he may be able to perform the advanced movements and eventually reach the upper levels. These exercises will also clearly show the horse's strong and weak attributes.

For the canter, the work-study will be similar to the transitions. At first whenever there is a change of direction at the tangent point between the two circles, the rider should demand a downward transition through the trot and then through the walk before switching leads, i.e., a simple change of lead. Later, as the counter-canter is confirmed, the rider should maintain the same lead as she changes circles.

The zigzag will be the same as practiced at the walk and trot, but the rider should act with more determination when moving the horse's shoulders left for the right lead and right for the left lead. The lengthening and the shortening will be the same as practiced at both the walk and trot. Moving the haunches at the canter should be performed only toward the cantering lead. Attempting to move the haunches toward the opposite side of the lead will most likely disunite the canter.

LESSON FIVE

On the Bit

I did not mention this part earlier because when a horse is performing all the exercises properly, he should come on the bit on his own. In 1921, the *Federation Equestre Internationale* (F.E.I.) was founded and published the English version of the rule book in which the expression "on the bit" first appeared.

What does "on the bit" mean? While research does not give any clue to the expression's origin, research does indicate that "on the bit" is a loose translation of the French expression *mise en main*, which translated literally would mean placing in hand. Perhaps a more precise and accurate expression would be *dans la main*, which translates to "in the hand." But the expression "on the bit" already has taken a life of its own.

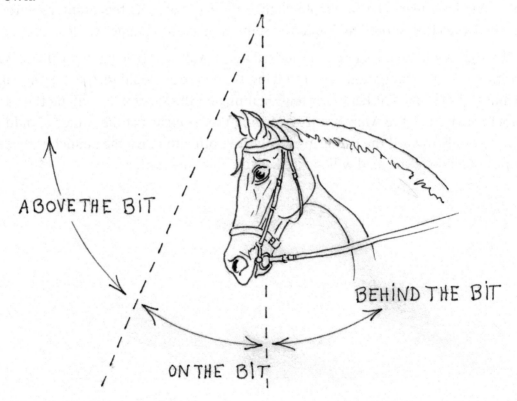

Figure 53 – On the bit

While habit and custom have left riders with this nebulous expression, which tends to create more problems than solutions, it may be helpful to explain its function and purpose. "In the hand," or the more common "on the bit," is the flexion of the horse's neck in impulsion. In flexion, the horse's top line and neck muscles are becoming round and stretched characterized by the fixity of the horse's head supported by a neck without stiffness. "In the hand" is an easy attitude that is variable and is also a function of the horse's conformation and on the level of training. The horse's neck should be rounded with the poll at the highest point, and his nose should be on a vertical line from the ground or slightly in front of the vertical. The horse's mouth should be soft and in constant contact with the rider's polite hands. The contact must always be the consequence of the horse's impulsion and not the action of the rider's pulling hands. Scientific study indicates that with impulsion, the horse's top line muscles (*dorso-lumbar*) become stretched contributing to the elevation and roundness of the neck when supported by engagement of the hindquarters.

What is the purpose of the horse being on the bit (in the hand)?

When the horse is "on the bit, " training is facilitated by:

1. Rendering the horse obedient to the rider 's slightest demand;
2. Providing proper head carriage,
3. Paralyzing the horse's defenses,
4. Allowing and facilitating any changes of balance, gaits and speed,
5. Softening and activating the horse's top line,
6. Rendering the horse more attentive and becoming less shy.

• Nota Bene •

At liberty, most horses naturally balance themselves. When horses are ridden, the disturbances from the rider's weight create unbalance, muscle contractions, resistances, and sometimes, retaliations. Riding the horse on the bit will minimize these inconveniences and even eliminate them.

How does the rider establish her horse to be "on the bit?"

Since virtually all horse's tensions (contractions) manifest in his mouth [or jaw], the rider ought to soften the horse's mouth with cessions and flexions.

What is a cession or flexion of the mouth?

A cession of the mouth is when the horse yields his jaws and softens the mouth. It is conceptualized by a quiet chewing on the bit (the horse is said to become "talkative"). The horse becomes very soft in the rider's hand.

How does the rider soften the horse's mouth?

The cession of the mouth can be obtained as follows:

- The rider should progressively increase the rein tension on the bit, accompanied by slowly elevating her hands vertically.

- The rider should gently lift the horse's neck until he carries his own head high and slightly opens his mouth. Then, the horse will flex at the poll and begin chewing on the bit. The horse will become very soft in the rider's hands.

- The rider should then release the tension on the reins by lowering her hands (called "descent of the hand").

Every time the horse immobilizes or stiffens his mouth the rider should repeat the same action. If the horse still resists, displacing the haunches will remedy the matter.

What is a flexion of the neck?

A flexion is an elevation of the horse's neck and a closing of the neck and head angle. The horse's forehead is on a vertical line from the ground while the poll remains the highest point.

There are two types of flexions:

- Lateral and
- Direct

A. Lateral Flexion

Lateral flexion is a slight rotation of head horse's head to the left (or to the right) around the two first cervical vertebrae (*Atlas* and *Axis*), to stretch and unlock the muscles on either side of the poll. These flexions will be followed by yielding of the jaws (the horse chewing quietly on the bit).

How does the rider demand a lateral flexion?

1. For a left lateral flexion, the rider should act with a slight left "direct rein" to bring the horse's head to the left.

2. The rider should close her left leg at the girth.

3. The rider should close the fingers of both hands to incite the horse to yield his jaws.

4. If necessary, the rider should vibrate the rein a few times with the opposite hand, i.e., the rider should vibrate the right rein if the left lateral flexion is demanded. (A vibration on the rein is similar to the tremolo of the violin player.)

5. At the slightest yielding of the jaws, the rider should immediately reward the horse by lowering the hand and softening the contact with the horse's mouth.

6. The rider should caress the horse as a reward, in order to confirm that the yielding of the horse was the rider's wish.

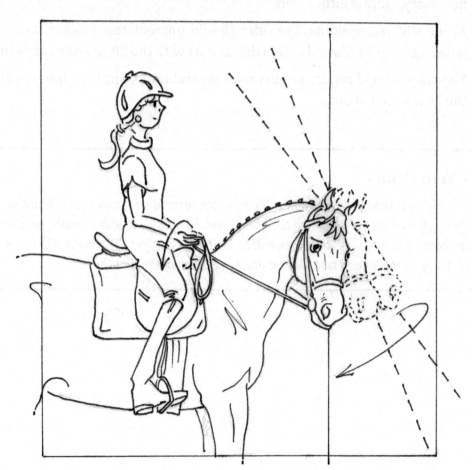

Figure 54 – Lateral flexion

B.   Direct Flexion

A direct flexion is a longitudinal rotation of the neck at the poll followed by a yielding of the jaws. The horse chewing on the bit will relax his mouth. The horse's neck, elevated and round, remains in the axis of the horse's body.

How does the rider demand a direct flexion?

1. The rider should slowly and vertically elevate the horse's neck and head by gently lifting both hands.

2. The rider should close both legs.

3. The rider should simultaneously tighten her fingers on both reins, and, if necessary, vibrate either rein.

4. At the slightest yielding, the rider should immediately reward the horse by lowering both hands and soften the contact with the bit (descent of the hands).

5. The rider should repeat the demand several times until the horse maintains the flexion on his own.

• *Nota Bene* •

Flexions should be asked initially from the ground and then while mounted. By slowly and tactfully turning the horse's head from side to side to make believe the horse is saying, "no," the horse will be invited to say, "yes." The horse will begin chewing on the bit and relax his mouth, i.e., cession of the mouth.

Figure 55 – Direct flexion

Figure 56 – Is my horse on the bit?

When the horse has learned what is being asked in the lateral and direct flexion, the rider should practice them to properly position and stabilize the horse's head. While working at the walk for a period of time, the rider should demand the flexions every time the horse is not on the bit. Also, the rider should spend time to develop the horse's neck muscles. At the trot, the rider should be demanding a series of lateral and direct flexions which gradually will develop the neck muscles and maintain the horse on the bit.

C. Placing the Horse on the Bit

If the horse does not naturally come on the bit and round his top line, there are several exercises that can be practiced to achieve this result. The exercises should be first be practiced at the walk in both directions.

A. Working on a circle to the right, the rider should allow the horse to carry himself by rounding his top line and maintaining his balance.

1. While sustaining a regular walk that is not too fast or too slow, the rider softens the contact with the bit but maintains the horse's head with his poll being the highest part of his body (*see light half-halts*).

2. The rider acts with her inside leg closer to the girth (propulsive aid) and the outside leg slightly back (position-regulating-passive) and asks the horse to displace his body to the outside, i.e., to the left.

The horse may slightly veer laterally to the outside, and should round his body around the rider's inside leg, lift his back, and round his top line, thereby coming on the bit. The rider should repeat the exercise tracking to the left.

• *Nota Bene* •

The rider must remember that the horse must balance himself. The rider should maintain the same walk with the reins sufficiently long to allow the horse to properly place his body.

D. Placing the Horse on the Bit While Moving Laterally

The rider should begin this exercise after having unlocked the horse's poll by means of the lateral and direct flexions while at the halt and then at the walk and trot, on a circle tracking to the left or to the right,

1. In cadence/tempo with the walk, the rider opens and closes her fingers on her inside hand.

2. The rider acts with her inside leg at the girth until the horse has given a slight inside lateral flexion.

3. The actions should be repeated until the horse can maintain a constant head position.

When the horse has learned what is being asked of him and easily comes on the bit, the exercise should be repeated in both directions at the walk, then at trot and canter.

The key to this exercise is that while the rider is acting with her inside hand by opening and closing her fingers on the rein, the rider's hands must never move backward and pull on the horse's mouth. The idea is to push the horse's body toward his head instead of pulling the horse's head toward his body.

The proper leg aids push the horse toward a steady hand that receives the flexion. To place himself properly, the horse must propel himself and be balanced in his natural attitude. The rider must soften her aids as soon as the horse has yielded so that the horse does not learn to lean on the rider's hands and acquire a bad habit of pulling.

• Nota Bene •

When the rider acts with her inside leg near the girth, the rider displaces the horse's body toward the outside of the circle. As the horse veers away from the circle, the rider should feel the horse's back lifting and rounding with the horse placing himself on the bit. The rider should also feel that the horse becomes lighter in her hands. As soon as the horse is in the proper position, the .rider should cease her hand and leg actions but remain vigilant and be ready to repeat the leg and hand actions whenever the horse loses the proper head position, hollows his back, or resists.

To stimulate the horse to come on the bit, the rider should begin walking the horse on a straight line. The rider should be sitting in a correct erect upper body position with her hands positioned low, i.e., level with the horse's withers, and her legs positioned under her seat. The rider acts with both legs to solicit the horse to stretch his neck to come in contact with her steady hands, give a cession of the mouth, yield at the poll, and engage his hindquarters so that he will lift and round his back, i.e., his top line.

• Nota Bene •

The rider must stimulate the horse forward with her legs toward her steady hands and never pull back on the horse's head. When the rider's reins are too long, the rider's first reaction will be to move her hands backward and thereby engage in pulling. To avoid this mistake, the rider should adjust both reins and squeeze her elbows against her hips to aid her in acquiring the proper position.

An anecdote from history might help the rider to remember these simple rules. While on his deathbed, F. Baucher was being assisted by his friend and student General L'Hotte. To impart some advice, M. Baucher grabbed the General's hand in his own and said, "When you ride a horse you must do this," as M. Baucher squeezed the General's fingers with a steady hand, "and not do that" as General L'Hotte pulled back his hand.

LESSON SIX

Practical Exercises

The following exercises, combining all the horse's body parts, were designed to improve obedience to the rider's aids. The longitudinal and lateral movements further develop impulsion, flexibility, engagement, balance and harmony in general.

To better explain the following figures, some kind of enclosure such as a Dressage arena or a *manège* may be used. But in fact all these patterns could be practiced anywhere.

• Nota Bene •

The word "dressage" originates from the French verb, dresser, *meaning "to teach," but in the world of horses, it is now used to mean "to train." When Dressage is capitalized, it implies showing; dressage with a lower case "d" indicates training.*

Manège (a word of Italian origin and adopted by the French) is an indoor arena that can be considered as the equivalent of a gymnasium where horses and riders are trained.

After undergoing many changes in dimensions, Dressage arenas now are consistently found in two sizes: 40 meters in length and 20 meters in width (131 feet x 66 feet) for the lower levels, and 60 meters in length and 20 meters in width (197 feet x 66 feet)) for the upper and F.E.I. levels. To be able to follow precise patterns easily, letters have been arranged around the entire perimeter. (After undergoing many changes, the letters are well settled today and are universal.)

For the smaller arena, letters A, K, E, H, C, M, B, and F are placed around the perimeter, and the center line is designated with the letters D, X, and G.

The origin of the sequence of letters around the Dressage arena remains a mystery. These letters are thought to have appeared during the first Dressage competition in the year 1912. One can speculate why these letters were chosen. A common belief is that these letters were used to designate the German Cavalry barracks with 60 x 20 meter areas in between the barracks.

One of the many mnemonics that have been suggested to remember the sequence is: **All K**ing **E**douard's **H**orses **C**an **M**ake **B**ig **F**ences.

For the large arena, letters A, K, V, E, S, H, C, M, R, B, P, and F are placed around the perimeter, and letters D, L, X, I, and G designate the center line.

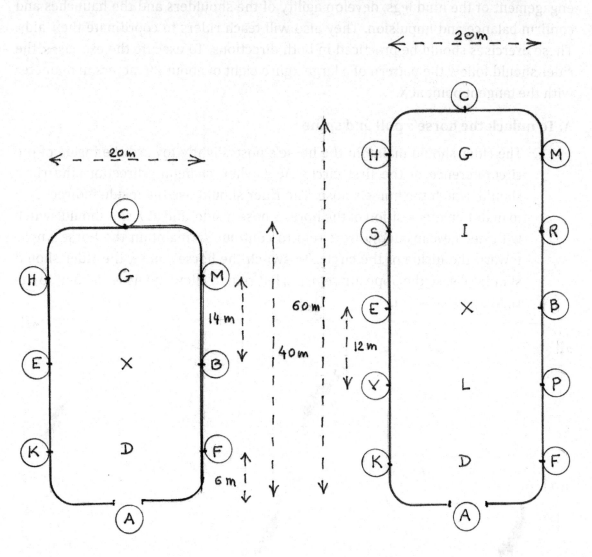

Figure 57 – Dressage arenas

Exercises

Although the following basic exercises should first be demanded at the walk so that horse and rider can learn how to proceed, the real training work will always be executed at the trot and canter. These exercises were designed to improve the horse's engagement of the hind legs, develop agility of the shoulders and the haunches and confirm balance and impulsion. They also will teach riders to coordinate their aids. These exercises should be practiced in both directions. To execute the exercises, the rider should follow the pattern of a large figure eight of about 20 meters in diameter with the tangent point at X.

A. To unlock the horse's poll and spine

1. The rider should maintain the horse's nose slightly toward the inside of the circumference of the first circle. At X when changing direction, the rider should switch the horse's nose. The rider should use the inside indirect rein to maintain the position of the horse's nose inside, and at X she should switch with her new inside indirect rein to continue to maintain the horse's nose toward the inside of the circle. To switch the horse's nose, the rider should simply release the opposite rein, i.e., left rein to allow the nose to point to the right and vice versa.

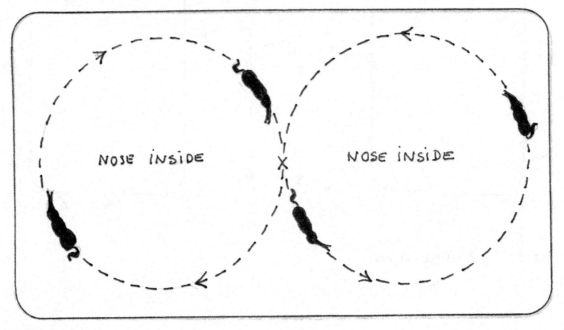

NOSE INSIDE   NOSE INSIDE

Figure 58 – Nose in

2. The rider should follow the figure eight maintaining the horse's nose to the
   outside and changing the bend at X to the new outside. The rider's aids should
   be outside indirect rein.

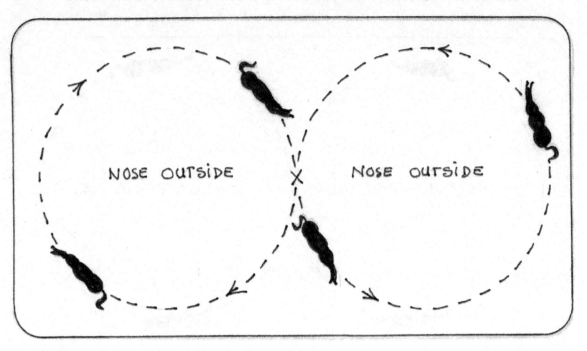

Figure 59 – Nose out

3. Every half circle throughout the figure eight, the rider should alternate the horse's nose position from inside to outside. The rider should switch from using the inside indirect rein (to position the horse's nose inside) to the outside indirect rein (when positioning the horse's nose to the outside).

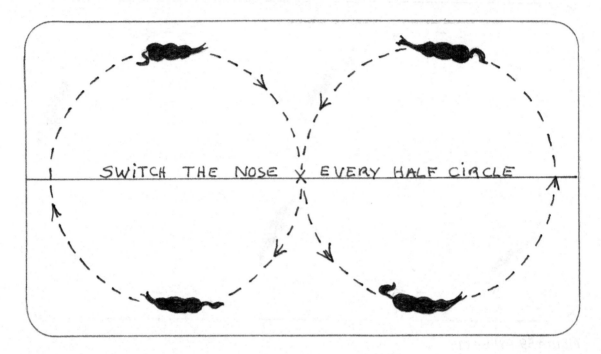

Figure 60 – Nose in and out

B. To prepare for the rotation of the shoulders around the haunches:

From the long side of the track, the rider should ask the horse to make a quarter turn toward the inside of the arena by pivoting the horse's shoulders around the haunches. After perpendicularly crossing the entire arena, the rider should asked the horse to perform another quarter turn to rejoin the track, but this time it should be in the opposite direction (if the first quarter turn is to the right the next one should be to the left or vice versa). Initially, the quarter turn should be performed with a counter bend (turn to the right with the horse's nose to the left or vice versa). In the future, to better prepare for the true pirouette, the bend should be toward the direction of the turn (i.e., turn to the right with the nose to the right).

The same exercise should also be demanded by moving the haunches a quarter turn around the shoulders.

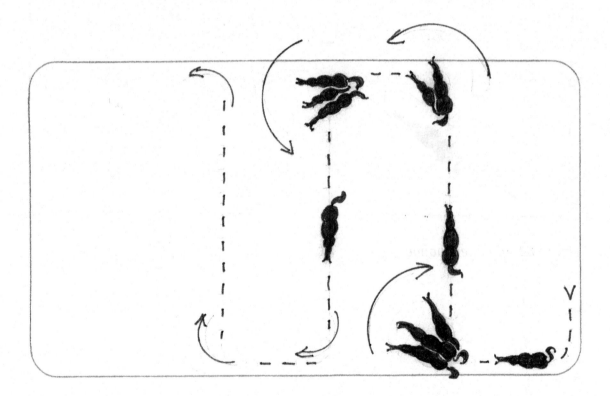

Fig 61 – Preparing for rotation around the haunches

121

C. To stretch and compress the horse's entire body

Lengthen and shorten the gaits following the pattern of a counter change of direction. For the first element of the counter change, the rider should demand an increase of speed, ride the turn by pushing the horse's shoulders toward the new direction, and then reduce the speed for the second element. The opposite should also be demanded, i.e., move slowly through the first portion and move forward through the second portion.

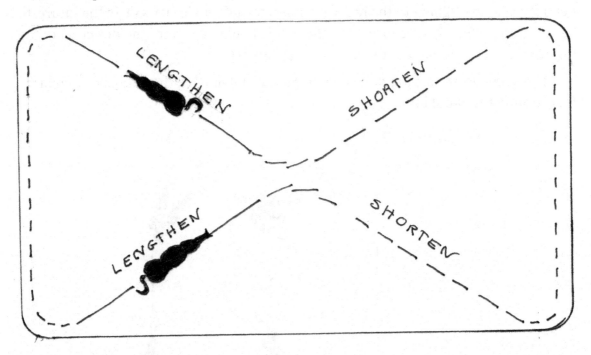

Figure 62 – Counter change

D. To further unlock the horse's shoulders

1. From the reference circle the rider should spiral in, acting with an outside direct rein,

2. The rider should spiral out, with an inside indirect rein to push the shoulders.

The rider should move only the horse's forehand.

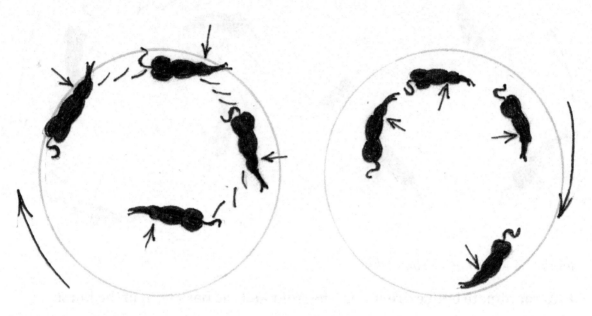

Figure 63 – Unlocking the shoulders

E. To further unlock the horse's haunches

1. From the reference circle, the rider should spiral in, acting with an outside leg behind the girth.
2. The rider should spiral out, with an inside leg behind the girth to push the haunches.

The rider should primarily move the back end of the horse.

Figure 64 – Pushing the haunches

F. To coordinate both extremities [the front and the back end] of the horse

From the reference circle, the rider should spiral in, simultaneously pushing the shoulders and the haunches toward the inside (outside indirect rein and outside leg behind the girth.)

The rider should spiral out by reversing the aids (inside indirect rein and inside leg behind the girth), to push the entire horse's body toward the original perimeter of the reference circle.

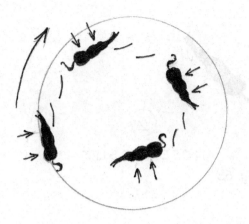

Figure 65 – Moving shoulders and haunches

G. To individually and then simultaneously move the horse's body parts

The rider should follow the pattern of a tight serpentine throughout the entire arena, from track to track, making as many loops as possible. For each set of loops:

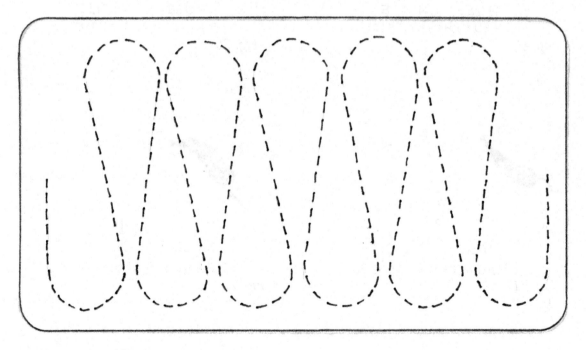

Figure 66 – Serpentine

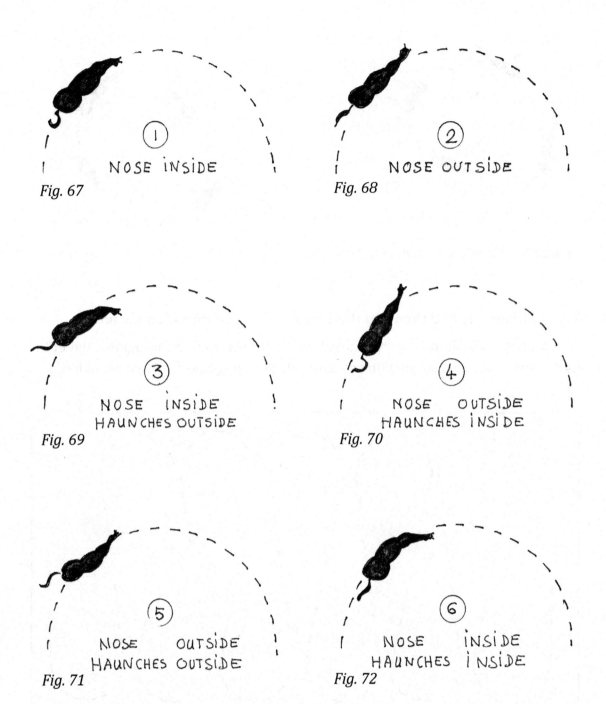

1. NOSE INSIDE

Fig. 67

2. NOSE OUTSIDE

Fig. 68

3. NOSE INSIDE
HAUNCHES OUTSIDE

Fig. 69

4. NOSE OUTSIDE
HAUNCHES INSIDE

Fig. 70

5. NOSE OUTSIDE
HAUNCHES OUTSIDE

Fig. 71

6. NOSE INSIDE
HAUNCHES INSIDE

Fig. 72

1. The rider should turn the horse's nose inside, using an inside direct rein (or indirect rein if the horse falls toward the inside). *(Fig. 67)*

2. The rider should turn the horse's nose outside, using an outside indirect rein. *(Fig. 68)*

3. The rider should turn the horse's nose inside and push the haunches outside, using direct rein and an inside leg behind the girth. *(Fig. 69)*

4. The rider should turn the horse's nose outside and push the haunches inside, using an outside indirect rein and an outside leg behind the girth. *(Fig. 70)*

5. The rider should turn the horse's nose outside and the haunches outside, using an outside indirect rein and an inside leg behind the girth. *(Fig. 71)*

6. The rider should turn the horse's nose inside and the haunches inside, using an inside direct rein and an outside leg behind the girth. *(Fig. 72)*

Every five strides the rider should alternate the horse's bend from the inside to the outside, acting with indirect rein of opposition and a coordinating leg behind the girth on the same side as the bend.

H. To coordinate the rider's aids by displacing the horse's body parts

1. On the diagonal F to X, the rider should maintain the horse's body parallel to the long side of the arena (right indirect rein and right leg behind the girth).

2. At X, the rider should turn the horse to the right and ride a 10 meter circle to the right to re-activate the horse's hind legs,

3. From X to H, the rider should follow the next diagonal segment pushing the horse's shoulders and haunches equally and simultaneously.

The rider should proceed in the same manner on the next diagonal from K to X. At X, the rider should perform a 10-meter circle to the left, and from X to M the rider should finish the remainder of the diagonal.

Figure 73 – Coordinating the rider's aids

I. To supple the horse's spinal column and to teach the rider to coordinate the aids

1. On the diagonal from F to X the rider should push the shoulders and the haunches equally to the left (right indirect rein and right leg behind the girth).

2. At X the rider should lead the horse on a 10-meter circle to the right.

3. On the return to X, the rider should change the horse's bend and immediately follow another 10-meter circle to the left (figure eight).

4. From X to M, the rider should push the shoulders and the haunches to the right (left indirect rein and left leg behind the girth).

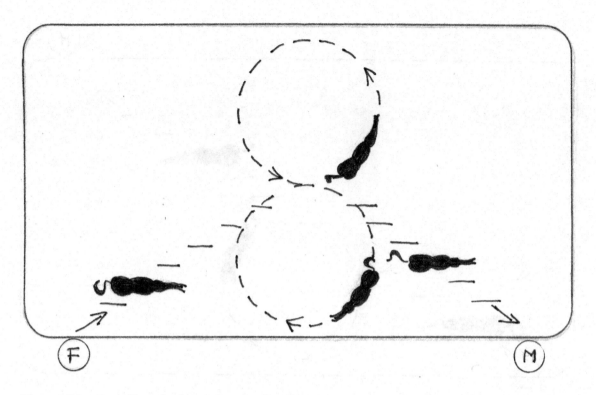

Figure 74 – Suppling the horse's spinal column

• *Nota Bene* •

On the circles, the rider should activate the trot while maintaining her inside leg near the girth for activity and her outside leg behind the girth for position to prevent the horse's haunches from drifting toward the outside of the circle.

J. To develop instantaneous response to the rider's aids

1. On the diagonal from F to X the rider should continue to move laterally to the left (right indirect rein and right leg behind the girth).
2. At X, the rider should circle to the right and immediately ask for a canter departure on the right lead.
3. At X, the rider should return to the trot and moving sideways again, finish the diagonal X to H.

The rider should proceed in the same manner on the following diagonal from K to X to M circling to the left at the canter.

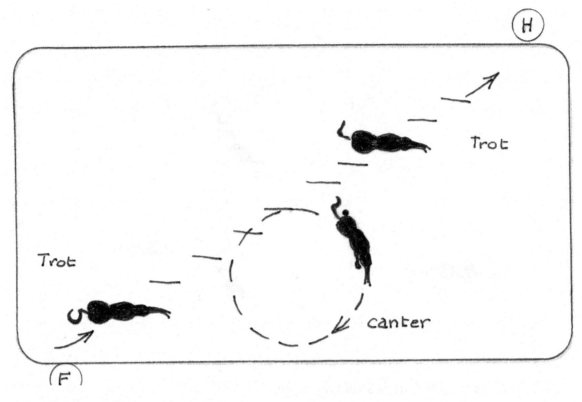

Figure 75 – Developing instantaneous response to the rider's aids

K. To further develop obedience and spontaneity to the rider's aids

1. On the long center line the rider should trot going straight from A to X.

2. At X the rider should circle right and immediately canter right.

3. At X the rider should ask for simple change of lead initially through a brief trot. When the horse is able, the rider should ask for a simple lead change through a brief walk, circle left, and immediately canter left.

4. At X complete the center line from X to C at the trot.

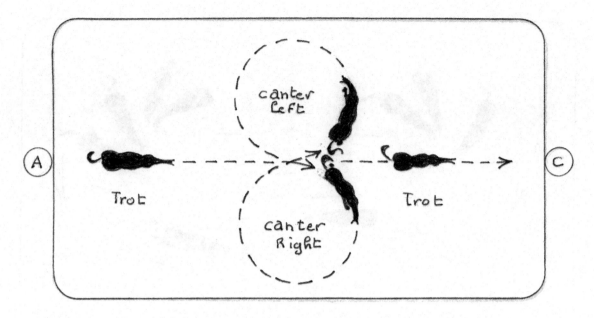

Figure 76 – Further developing obedience and spontaneity to the rider's aids

L. To improve the mobility of the horse's hindquarters and strengthen his stifle joints

Between the two quarter lines, the rider should follow the pattern of a figure eight with two half circles separated by two short diagonal lines. The rider should begin the exercise at the walk and later practice it at the trot. On the half circle, the rider, using an inside indirect rein and an inside leg behind the girth, should push the shoulders and the haunches toward the outside. At the next diagonal line, the rider should reverse her aids and proceed in the same manner moving laterally.

Figure 77 – Improving the mobility of the horse's hindquarters

M. To improve the suppleness of the horse's spinal column in both directions

1. At each cardinal point on the reference circle, the rider should walk and trot the pattern of four small circles toward the inside of the reference circle.

2. The rider should follow the pattern of 4 small circles toward the outside of the reference circle.

3. When both horse and rider are able to ride these circles without efforts, the rider should proceed in the same manner riding four consecutive figure eights at each cardinal point on the reference circle. To be able to ride the same size circles, the rider should count the strides throughout each revolutions to obtain the exact same number of strides for each individual circles. As the horse becomes more agile the diameter of these circles should gradually be reduced.

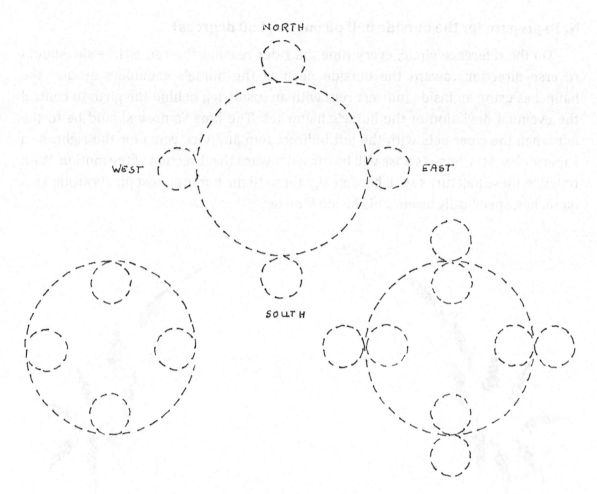

Figure 78 – Improving the suppleness of the horse's spinal column

---

• *Nota Bene* •

When the horse rotates his shoulders 360 degrees around his haunches from a stand-still, it is called a "turn on the haunches." When perform while in motion, at the walk, trot, and canter, it is called a "pirouette."

For a novice rider, the horse's nose could be placed toward the outside, but later, the nose MUST be placed toward the inside so that the horse can better pivot around his inside hind leg.

N. To prepare for the outside half pirouette (180 degrees)

On the reference circle, every time the rider reaches the center line she should reverse direction toward the outside pushing the horse's shoulders around the haunches using an inside indirect rein with an inside leg behind the girth to control the eventual deviation of the horse's haunches. The horse's nose should be to the left when the rider acts with the left indirect rein and vice versa for the right. At a superior level the horse's nose will be turned toward the direction of the motion. With practice, these half turns shall become tighter until the horse almost pivots around his haunches, specifically around his inside hind leg.

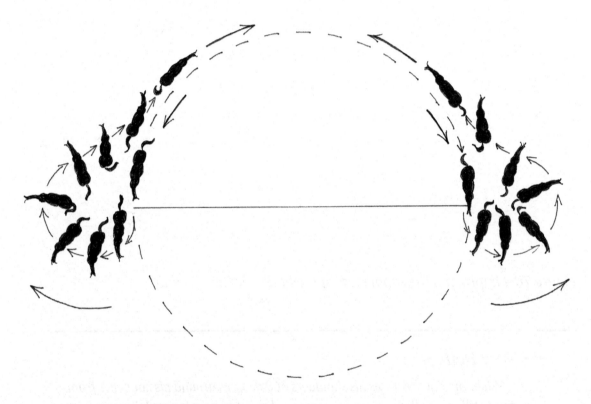

Figure 79 – Moving the haunches outside

• *Nota Bene* •

When the horse rotates his haunches 360 degrees around his shoulders from a standstill it is called a "turn on the forehand." When performed while in motion, at the walk and trot it is called a "counter-pirouette." It is extremely difficult to tightly execute this "counter-pirouette" at the canter, and it has been accomplished by only a few horses and riders.

For a novice rider, the nose could be on the same side as the acting leg behind the girth, but later, it must be positioned to the opposite side so that the horse can better pivot around the same side as the acting leg.

O. To prepare for the outside half counter pirouette

Each time the rider reaches the center line of the reference circle she should reverse direction toward the outside and push the horse's haunches around his shoulders.

The horse' nose should be on the same side as the acting leg behind the girth although at the superior level the horse's nose should be opposite to the active leg. With practice these half turns should become tighter until the horse almost pivots around his inside shoulder.

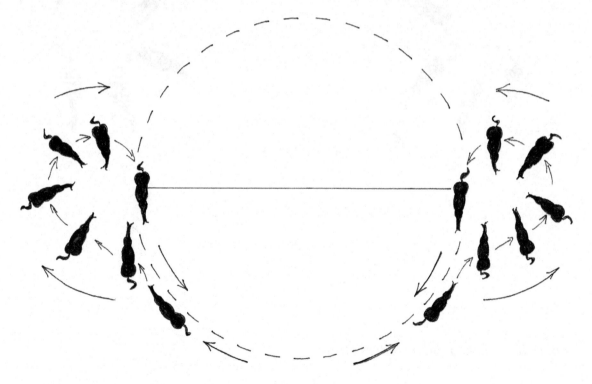

Figure 80 – Moving the haunches

P. To prepare for the inside half pirouette

Each time the rider reaches the center line of the reference circle, she should reverse direction toward the inside and push the horse's shoulders around his haunches.

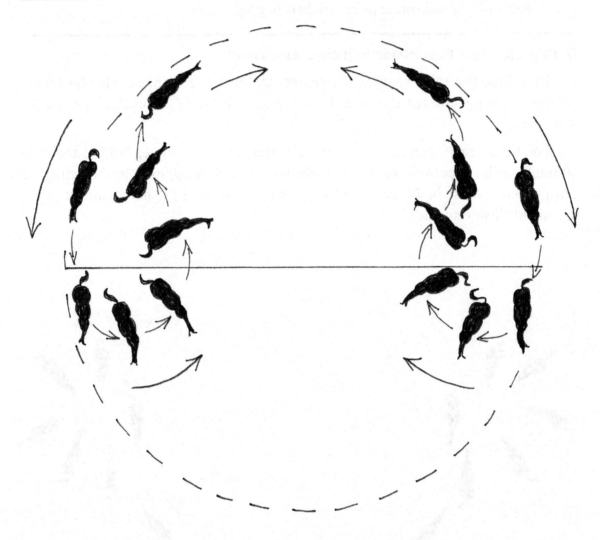

Figure 81 – Moving the shoulders inside

Q. To prepare for the inside half counter pirouette

Each time the rider reaches the center line of the reference circle, she should reverse direction toward the inside and push the horse's haunches around the shoulders.

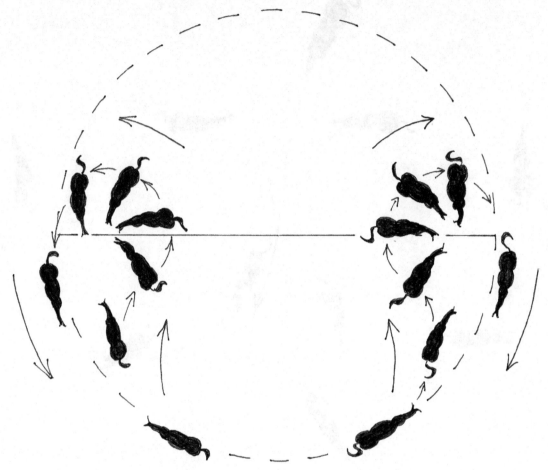

Figure 82 – Moving the haunches inside

R. To develop instantaneous obedience to the rider's aids and instill the idea of full pirouettes (360 degrees)

Each time the rider reaches the center line, she should follow the pattern of a small figure of eight and push the horse's shoulders slightly around the haunches toward the outside and then immediately toward the inside by simply reversing her aids. For now, the bend of the neck will remain on the same side as the indirect rein.

Figure 83 – Pushing the shoulders

S. To prepare for the instantaneous obedience to the rider's aids and eventually to perform full counter pirouettes

Each time the rider reaches the center line of the reference circle she should follow the pattern of a small figure eight by pushing the horse's haunches around the

138

shoulders toward the outside and then, as a variation, immediately push the haunches toward the inside simply by maintaining her aids. At the beginning the bend of the neck should remain on the same side as the leg acting behind the girth. In the future the bend of the neck should be toward the opposite side so that the horse is better able to pivot around the proper posterior, i.e., the one on the same side as the rider's acting leg behind the girth.

Figure 84 – Pushing the haunches

T. Test longitudinal obedience

At the walk, trot and ultimately at the canter, the rider should perform the following test around the entire arena:

1. At A stop, and then move forward,
2. At P ride a small circle slowing the pace,
3. At B stop, and move forward,
4. At R ride a large circle and lengthen the strides,
5. At C stop, and then move forward,
6. At S ride another small circle going slowly,
7. At E stop, and move forward,
8. At V ride another large circle lengthening the gait,
9. At A stop.

The rider should perform this exercise going two or three times around the arena before repeating the same work tracking in the other direction.

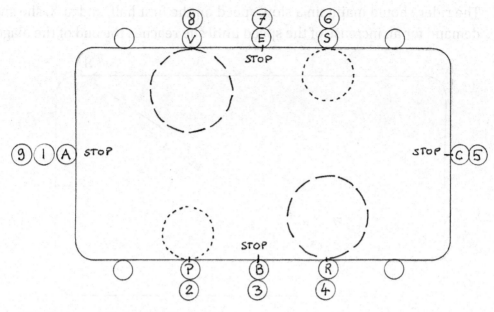

Figure 85 – Test on longitudinal obedience

U.   Lengthening the trot on the diagonals across the arena

To better prepare the horse to open and lengthen the trot throughout the long diagonal of the big Dressage arena, the rider should work in portions:

1. On the diagonal, the rider should incite her horse to lengthen the gait on the first half only. For the second half the rider should reduce speed.

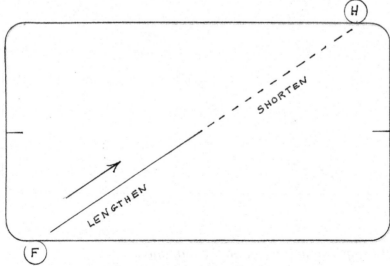

Figure 86 – (a) Lengthening the trot on the diagonals

2. The rider should maintain a slow speed on the first half, and at X, she should demand for an increase of the speed until she reaches the end of the diagonal.

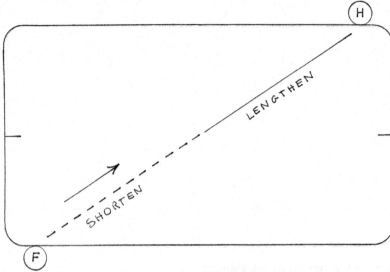

Figure 87 – (b) Lengthening the trot on the diagonals

3. Then the rider should increase speed only between the quarter lines.

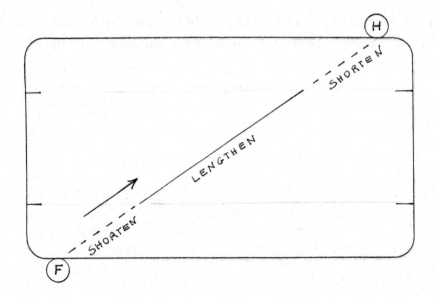

Figure 88 – (c) Lengthening the trot on the diagonals

142

4. The rider should increase speed during the first half, slow for just a few strides in the middle at X and ask the horse again to move out for the second half.

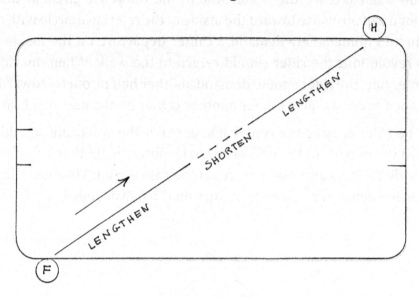

Figure 89 – (d) Lengthening the trot on the diagonals

With practice, the horse should easily be able to open the trotting strides across the entire diagonal.

• *Nota Bene* •

Two important tips in practicing these exercises are:

1. To stimulate the horse to exert more energy in the increase of speed, the rider should tactfully use her whip and clearly tap her horse on his shoulder.

2. To teach the horse to regain his equilibrium, the rider should demand for a halt at the end of each diagonal.

When the horse consistently demonstrates great energy in the lengthening, the action of the whip will no longer be necessary. The rider, however, should always ready to act should the horse fail to respond to the rider's legs. In the future, to prepare for competition, the rider should ask for a lengthening each time she crosses the arena's diagonal.

V. Improve canter departures

When the rider crosses the center line of the reference circle at the walk, she should ask for a half pirouette toward the inside of the reference circle with her outside indirect rein and immediately demand a canter departure on the inside lead. After one or two revolutions the rider should return to the walk. When the rider reaches the next center line, the rider should demand another half pirouette toward the inside of the reference circle and also ask for another canter on the new inside lead.

When the rider crosses the center line again at the walk, she should direct the horse toward the outside of the reference circle, perform another half pirouette, and immediately demand a canter departure on the inside lead. The rider should repeat this exercise and demand a canter departure on the new inside lead.

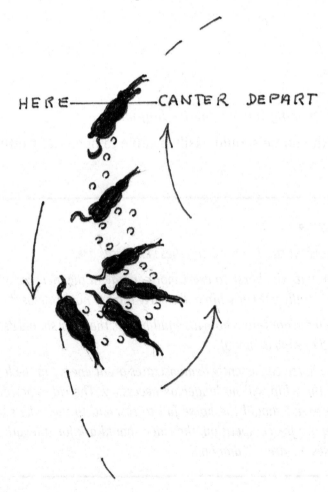

Figure 90 – Improving the canter departure

W. Spiral in and out at the canter

Part One

1. At the canter the rider should gradually spiral in from the reference circle.

2. When reaching the center of the reference circle she should return to the walk.

3. The rider should reverse direction, pushing the horse's shoulders around the haunches and tactfully lead the horse back to the reference circle,

4. Tracking in the opposite direction, the rider should ask for a canter departure and spiral toward the interior of the circle again,

5. When reaching the center of the reference circle, she should return to the walk.

6. The rider should reverse direction, and repeat the entire exercise.

Part Two

1. At the canter, the rider should maintain the canter while spiraling in and out several times from the reference circle and then return to the walk,

2. The rider should Reverse direction by rotating the shoulders around the haunches and immediately demand a canter departure,

3. The rider should repeat the spiraling in and out at the canter several times.

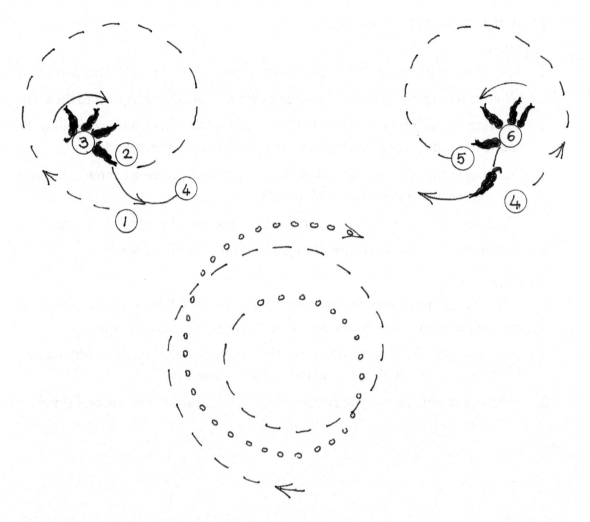

Figure 91 – Spiraling in and out at the canter

• *Nota Bene* •

Initially, the rider should perform wide spirals; later, when the horse is more capable, the spirals should become tighter.

X. To improve and perfect the counter-canter

1. At the counter-canter, when reaching the center of the reference circle, the rider should follow the pattern of a small circle to the outside and return to the counter-canter on the reference circle.

2. When the horse becomes more agile, the circle should be demanded toward the inside of the reference circle,

3. When able, the rider should lead the horse onto a small figure eight tangent to the reference circle.

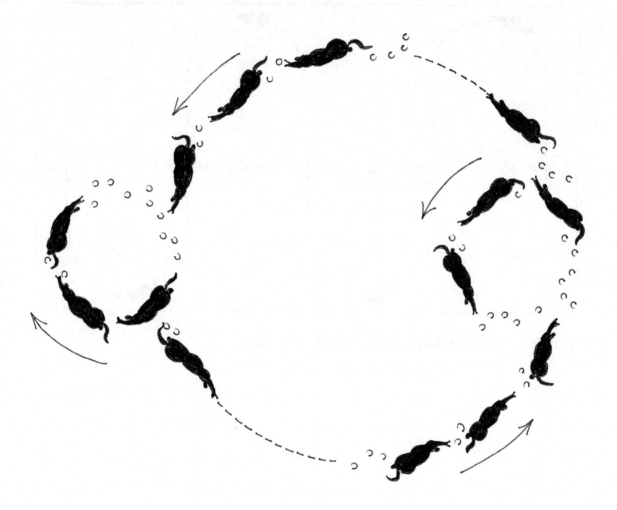

Figure 92 – Improving the counter-canter

147

Y. To prepare for the future flying changes of lead at the canter

At the canter, following the pattern of a wide serpentine with four loops, the rider should ask for a simple change through a trot each time she reaches the center line. When the horse has learned the exercise, the rider should try to obtain the simple changes through walk and then a stop. As the horse becomes more agile, the number of consecutive loops should be increased as the radius is decreased, i.e., the serpentine should become tighter.

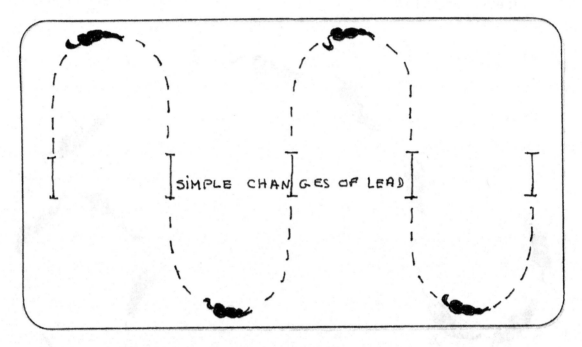

Figure 93 – Preparing for the future flying changes of lead

Z. Exercises blending longitudinal and lateral movements to verify the promptness of the horse's obedience and the rider's accuracy

These exercises should be demanded first at the walk and then at the trot.

1. At A from a halt, the rider should go large.

2. At P, the rider should complete small circle moving the horse's shoulders around his haunches.

3. At B, the rider should follow the pattern of a 10 meters circle while activating the gait.

4. At R, the rider should complete a small circle moving the horse's haunches around his shoulders.

5. At C the rider should bring the horse to a halt.

6. From H to X, the rider should move the entire horse's body, laterally.

7. At X, she should ride a 10 meters circle tangent to points E and X on the right lead canter.

8. From X to K, the rider should move the entire horse's body laterally.

9. At A, the rider should demand a halt.

10. The rider should move quietly at the chosen gait from A to F.

11. From F to X, the rider should lengthen the gait.

12. At X, the rider should shorten the gait for two or three strides.

13. From X to H, the rider should lengthen the strides.

14. At C, the rider should stop.

After giving a short break to the horse, the rider should repeat the same exercises tracking in the other direction.

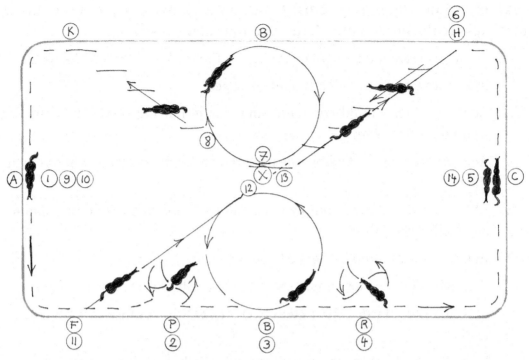

Figure 94 - Exercises blending longitudinal and lateral movements

• Nota Bene •

Leg yielding (also known as: cession to the leg) does not qualify as a true lateral movement even though the horse is crossing his front and back legs while moving sideways. The horse's spine is not bent. In the early twentieth century and even today, leg yielding has been introduced and dropped from Dressage tests repeatedly. An active debate persists regarding the usefulness of this exercise.

I have found the exercise to be acceptable, but it should be used primarily to teach the rider to properly apply the lateral aids, i.e. right indirect rein and right leg behind the girth or vice versa. For the horse, however, caution should be manifested to avoid intensive practice of the leg yield as it places the horse's body in an awkward position, i.e., his head is turned toward on one side, while his spine is straight and the haunches deviate toward the opposite side. Overly zealous practice can create more problems than solutions and could generate lameness. As my favorite veterinarian has always said, "Ninety percent of lameness occurrences in a horse are the result of defective riding."

It is important for the rider to study the pirouettes and the counter pirouettes to perfect the agility of the horse's front and hind legs. Because the horse will be compelled to burden his hind legs to generate the freedom to move his forelegs, the activity of the hind legs will be reduced. To reestablish the activity of the hind legs, the rider must also rotate the horse's haunches around the front legs. In this respect, one exercise complements the other.

Friendly Advice:

- Always begin a work-study by being absolutely certain about what the work program will be and what you expect to accomplish with your horse. The rider always must have a plan from the simple to the complex.

- Each day always proceed from the easiest to the hardest and from the known to the unknown.

- Always use the same aids to obtain the same effects.

- Never confuse the rider's lack of abilities with the horses ignorance or unwillingness.

- Never try to solve two problems at the same time.

- Always remember that horses are kind and docile animals. They are herbivores and therefore they are not predators. They are sensitive to good treatments, to the voice and caresses. Hitting horses does not render submissiveness but rather, it result in irritability and apprehension.

- Horses are capable of attention and reflections; sometimes a poorly executed exercise may be easier to perform the next day because it is better understood.

- An unsatisfied rider should never become brutal or angry. The rider should examine the situation with a positive attitude and solve the situation with calmness.

- Always bring the horse back to calmness if he loses it by returning to the walk or stopping.

- During the evolution of their education, certain horses may reach a plateau. Do not rush them but wait until they have fully absorbed the new material.

- Always remember to properly warm up the horse's body because the horse may have developed stiffness from the previous sessions.

- Always be concerned with the impulsion, and always maintain the horse in front of the legs.

- The rider should always be conscious of the horse's straightness and even tempo.

- Always be considerate enough to know when to interrupt a work-study when the horse fatigues to avoid spasms or cramps in the muscular system, which may lead to defenses and retaliations. Be sure to give frequent rest periods to the horse.

- Always preserve a light and even contact with the horse's mouth. This contact begins with reins properly adjusted by the rider and maintained taut by the horse's impulsion.

- Horse balance: the horse is said to be in balance when he is moving forward at the slightest indication of the rider's legs and slows or stop at the slightest indication of the rider's hands without force.

- Always **ACT** and do not **REACT**.

- To help a horse maintain the same speed, the formula is simple: ask the horse to change gaits and change speed many, many times.

- At first, the rider may not know why the horse is inconsistent in his pace, the rider should invite the horse to perform many transitions, so that the horse can better engage and propel himself with his hind legs. With daily practice of these transitions, the horse should gradually improve and begin to maintain the same speed. Proper impulsion is the answer.

- To help a horse travel straight, the formula is simple: ask the horse to turn several times to the right and a similar amount of times to the left.

- Each failure brings the rider closer to success.

- To progress, the Rider should look for perfection in the most simple and elementary movements.

- Any hand action should always be preceded by the leg action.

- The rider should always disassociate the aids – legs without hands and hands without legs.

- When riding and training a horse, one should always remember to maintain the soft hands of a Lady, the posture of a Queen, and the manners of a Gentleman.

EPILOGUE

The exercises that have been described should be practiced as often as possible at the walk, then at the trot, and finally, when learned satisfactorily, they can be practiced at the canter. At first, these exercises may seem difficult but when repeated and corrected, they become easy to perform. If difficulties or problems occur, the rider should never hesitate to re-visit Lesson One, Part One. These exercises should be executed accurately, even though in the beginning they may seem complicated. The ability to follow described patterns as precisely as possible teaches the rider to coordinate her aids, improve the horse's ability to perform, develop greater impulsion and perfect his balance. These exercises open the doors to the upper level movements to eventually reach "high school" dressage. To succeed, the rider must always persevere and remember that "overnight success" has always been preceded by days and weeks of failures. By remaining positive and persistent, each failure brings the rider closer to success.

Wisdom teaches us:
NO ONE IS PROTECTED FROM SUCCESS
Voila. This ends *Divide and Conquer Book One.*

To continue the training of your horse, *Divide and Conquer Book Two décortique* [disects/analyzes by taking apart] the F.E.I. movements.

XENOPHON PRESS LIBRARY

www.XenophonPress.com

Xenophon Press is dedicated to the preservation of classical equestrian literature. We bring both new and old works to English-speaking riders.

30 Years with Master Nuno Oliveira, Henriquet 2011

A New Method to Dress Horses, Cavendish 2016

A Rider's Survival from Tyranny, de Kunffy 2012

Another Horsemanship, Racinet 1994

Art of the Lusitano, Yglesias de Oliveira 2012

Austrian Art of Riding, Poscharnigg 2015

Baucher and His School, Decarpentry 2011

Classic Show Jumping: the de Nemethy Method, de Nemethy 2016

Divide and Conquer Books 1 & 2, Lemaire de Ruffieu 2016

Dressage in the French Tradition, Diogo de Bragança 2011

Dressage Principles Illuminated, Expanded Edition, de Kunffy 2017

École de Cavalerie Part II, Robichon de la Guérinière 1992, 2015

Equine Osteopathy: What the Horses Have Told Me, Giniaux 2014

François Baucher: The Man and His Method, Baucher/Nelson 2013

Great Horsewomen of the 19th Century in the Circus, Nelson 2015

Gymnastic Exercises for Horses Volume II, Eleanor Russell 2013

H. Dv. 12 Cavalry Manual of Horsemanship, Reinhold 2014

Handbook of Jumping Essentials, Lemaire de Ruffieu 2015

Handbook of Riding Essentials, Lemaire de Ruffieu 2015

Healing Hands, Giniaux, DVM 1998

Horse Training: Outdoors and High School, Beudant 2014

Learning to Ride, Santini 2016

Legacy of Master Nuno Oliveira, Millham 2013

Lessons in Lightness, Mark Russell 2016

Methodical Dressage of the Riding Horse, Faverot de Kerbrech 2010

Principles of Dressage and Equitation a.k.a. Breaking and Riding, Fillis 2016

Racinet Explains Baucher, Racinet 1997

Science and Art of Riding in Lightness, Stodulka 2015

The Art of Riding a Horse or Description of Modern Manege in Its Perfection, D'Eisenberg 2015

The Art of Traditional Dressage, Volume I DVD, de Kunffy 2013
The Ethics and Passions of Dressage Expanded Ed., de Kunffy 2013
The Forward Impulse, Santini 2016
The Gymnasium of the Horse, Steinbrecht 2011
The Horses, a novel, Elaine Walker 2015
The Italian Tradition of Equestrian Art, Tomassini 2014
The Maneige Royal, de Pluvinel 2010, 2015
The Portuguese School of Equestrian Art, de Oliveira/da Costa 2012
The Spanish Riding School & Piaffe and Passage, Decarpentry 2013
To Amaze the People with Pleasure and Delight, Walker 2015
Total Horsemanship, Racinet 1999
Training with Master Nuno Oliveira double DVD set, Eleanor Russell 2016
Truth in the Teaching of Master Nuno Oliveira, Eleanor Russell 2015
Wisdom of Master Nuno Oliveira, de Coux 2012

Available at www.XenophonPress.com

CPSIA information can be obtained
at www.ICGtesting.com
Printed in the USA
LVOW03*2305071216

516330LV00029B/583/P